The German Army 1939–45 (1)

Blitzkrieg

Nigel Thomas • Illustrated by Stephen Andrew

Series editor Martin Windrow

First published in Great Britain in 1997 by
Osprey Publishing, Midland House, West Way,
Botley, Oxford OX2 0PH, UK
443 Park Avenue South, New York, NY 10016, USA
Email: info@ospreypublishing.com

© 1997 Osprey Publishing Ltd.

All rights reserved. Apart from any fair dealing for the purpose of private study,
research, criticism or review, as permitted under the Copyright, Designs and
Patents Act, 1988, no part of this publication may be reproduced, stored in a
retrieval system, or transmitted in any form or by any means electronic,
electrical, chemical, mechanical, optical, photocopying, recording or otherwise,
without the prior written permission of the copyright owner. Enquiries should
be addressed to the Publishers.

CIP Data for this publication is available from the British Library

ISBN 978-1-85532-639-2

Series Editor: MARTIN WINDROW

Military Editor: Sharon van der Merwe
Design: The Black Spot

Filmset in Singapore by Pica Ltd.
Printed in China through World Print Ltd.

06 07 08 09 10   19 18 17 16 15 14 13 12 11 10

FOR A CATALOGUE OF ALL BOOKS PUBLISHED BY
OSPREY MILITARY AND AVIATION PLEASE CONTACT:

NORTH AMERICA
Osprey Direct, C/o Random House
Distribution Center, 400 Hahn Road,
Westminster, MD 21157, USA
E-mail: info@ospreydirect.com

ALL OTHER REGIONS
Osprey Direct UK, P.O. Box 140,
Wellingborough, Northants, NN8 2FA, UK
E-mail: info@ospreydirect.co.uk

www.ospreypublishing.com

Dedication

This book is respectfully dedicated to my late father, War Substantive Lieutenant William Rowland Thomas, Royal Fusiliers, and the late Oberfeldarzt a.D. Dr. Med. Friedrich Herrmann, formerly of *198. Infanteriedivision* and the *Bundeswehr* – two men from whom I have learnt a lot.

Acknowledgements

This book would not have been possible without the generous help of many people, especially Mark Axworthy, Phillip Buss (MA), Josef Charita, Brian Davis, Dr. Friedrich Herrmann, David Littlejohn, Pierre C.T. Verheye and Stephen Andrew. The author would like to thank his family, Heather, Alexander and Dominick, for their continued support and encouragement.

Artist's Note

Readers may care to note that the original paintings from which the colour plates in this book were prepared are available for private sale. All reproduction copyright whatsoever is retained by the Publishers. All enquiries should be addressed to:

Stephen Andrew, 87 Ellisland, Kirkintilloch, Glasgow G66 2UA

The Publishers regret that they can enter into no correspondence upon this matter.

GERMAN ARMY 1939–45 (1) BLITZKRIEG

THE RECORD OF THE WEHRMACHT

On 30 January 1933 Adolf Hitler dismantled the Weimar Republic and established the Third Reich, with himself as *Führer* (leader) and head of state. On 15 March 1935 he abolished Weimar's armed forces, the *Reichswehr*, and replaced them with the *Wehrmacht*. Hitler announced that the Wehrmacht would not be bound by the restrictions imposed on the Reichswehr by the 1919 Treaty of Versailles, which limited it to 100,000 volunteers with no tanks, heavy artillery, submarines or aircraft.

The Wehrmacht expanded rapidly. On 1 September 1939, when Germany attacked Poland, it numbered 3,180,000 men. It eventually expanded to 9,500,000, and on 8/9 May 1945, the date of its unconditional surrender on the Western and Eastern Fronts, it still numbered 7,800,000. The Blitzkrieg period, from 1 September 1939 to 25 June 1940, was 10 months of almost total triumph for the Wehrmacht, as it defeated every country, except Great Britain, that took the field against it.

THE HIGH COMMAND OF THE ARMY AND THE WEHRMACHT

Hitler believed, incorrectly as events were to prove, that his political skills were matched by a unique ability as a strategic commander. His increasing influence on the Wehrmacht's conduct of the Second World War eventually proved to be disastrous.

As head of state, Hitler occupied the nominal position of *Oberster Befehlshaber der Wehrmacht* (Supreme Commander of the Armed Forces), and on 4 February 1938 he took over the most important professional position of *Oberbefehlshaber der Wehrmacht* (Commander of the Armed Forces), having forced his former protégé, Generalfeldmarschall Werner von Blomberg, to retire. Hitler held this post until his suicide on 30 April 1945, assisted by the subservient Generaloberst (later Generalfeldmarschall) Wilhelm von Keitel as *Chef des Oberkommandos der Wehrmacht* (Chief of Staff of the Armed Forces). Real power rested with Generalmajor (eventually Generaloberst) Alfred Jodl, technically Keitel's assistant as *Chef der Wehrmachtführungsamt* (Chief of the Operations Staff).

Germany, April 1934. An Obergefreiter, Oberschütze, Schütze and Gefreiter, all NCO candidates in service uniform, show the new Wehrmacht eagle on their M1916 helmets. They wear M1920 (eight-button) and M1928 (six-button) service tunics, M1920 rank insignia and M1928 marksmanship awards. (Brian Davis Collection)

10th Infantry Division in parade uniforms march past German officers, and Austrian officers absorbed into the German Army. The Austrian officers are wearing their M1933 *Bundesheer* uniforms with German breast eagles, and the characteristic Austrian *képi*. Vienna, March 1938. (Brian Davis Collection)

The Wehrmacht was divided into three arms – the Army (*Heer*), Navy (*Kriegsmarine*) and Air Force (*Luftwaffe*). The Army was the largest arm, averaging about 75% of total Wehrmacht strength, with 2,700,000 troops in September 1939, reaching a maximum strength of about 5,500,000, with 5,300,000 in May 1945.

Oberbefehlshaber des Heeres (Chief of the Army High Command) until 19 December 1941, when Hitler dismissed him and took over his post, was Generaloberst (later Generalfeldmarschall) Walther von Brauchitsch, assisted by General der Artillerie (later Generaloberst) Franz Halder as *Chef des Generalstabes des Heeres* (Chief of the Army General Staff). The Waffen-SS, formally established on 1 December 1939, was never technically part of the Wehrmacht, but it came under the control of the Army High Command.

The branches of the Army

On mobilisation on 26 August 1939 the Army was divided into the *Feldheer* (Field Army), advancing to attack the enemy, and the *Ersatzheer* (Replacement Army), remaining in Germany in support. The Field Army constituted three types of troops. Firstly, *Fechtende Truppen*, or combat troops, comprised Staffs (Armed Forces and Army High Commands; General Staff; Army Group, Army and Corps Staffs), Infantry (line, motorised, light and mountain), commando and penal units; Mobile Troops (cavalry, armour, mechanised infantry, reconnaissance and anti-tank units), Artillery, Engineers, Signals and Field Security Police Officials. Secondly, *Versorgungstruppen*, or Supply Troops, included Transport, Medical, Veterinary and Guard units, Military Police and Field Post Officials. Thirdly, *Sicherungstruppen* – Security Troops – were composed of Rear-Area commanders, second-line 'territorial rifle' (*Landesschützen*) battalions and prisoner-of-war camps. There were also Army Officials (including Chaplains), Bandmaster-Officers and Specialists (*Sonderführer*).

The organisation of the Field and Replacement Armies

The largest wartime Field Army units had no fixed organisation. There were five army groups: two (*Nord* and *Süd*) for the Polish campaign, and three more (A-C) for the Western campaigns. Each Army Group (*Heeresgruppe*) was composed of two or three armies with perhaps 400,000 men. There were 14 armies, each Army (*Armee*) comprising three or four corps with about 200,000 men, and, from June 1940, two reinforced Armoured Corps, called *Panzergruppe* or Armoured Groups (*von Kleist* and *Guderian*) each one controlling three motorised corps. There were 33 corps (1-13,17,21,23-30,38,40,42-4,46-9), each Corps (*Korps*) with two to five infantry divisions and perhaps 60,000 men; and seven motorised corps, each Motorised Corps (*Korps(mot.)*) with two or three armoured and motorised divisions, and one (XV) with three light divisions. One cavalry division and the four mountain divisions came directly under the control of their respective armies.

During the Blitzkrieg period 143 infantry divisions were formed, their quality depending on the 'Wave' (*Welle*), to which they belonged. In addition to the 35 well-established peacetime 1st Wave divisions (1-46 series), there were divisions of elderly veterans or untrained reservists or recruits hastily assembled from occupied Poland and Czechoslovakia, as well as the nine Replacement Divisions (*Ersatzdivisionen*) of the 10th Wave (270-280 series). Each infantry division (*Infanteriedivision*) of 16,977 men was made up of three infantry regiments plus divisional support units: one four-battalion artillery regiment; a reconnaissance battalion, with mounted, bicycle and support squadrons; an anti-tank battalion; an engineer battalion; a signals battalion; and divisional

An Unteroffizier of the 67th Infantry Regiment in Ruhleben, near Berlin, 1938 wearing the M1935 undress uniform, with the peaked cap usually worn by NCOs, with this uniform. He is instructing recruits, dressed in M1933 fatigue uniforms, in rifle drill with Karabiner 98k rifles. Note the typical soiled and crumpled appearance of the fatigue uniforms. (Brian Davis Collection)

services – up to ten motorised and horsedrawn transport columns; a medical company, a motorised field hospital and veterinary company; a Military Police Troop and a Field Post Office.

An infantry regiment with 3,049 men (*Infanterieregiment*) had three infantry battalions, a 180-strong infantry gun company and a 170-strong anti-tank company. A battalion (*Bataillon*) of 860 men had three rifle companies and a 190-strong machine gun (actually a support) company. A 201-strong rifle company (*Schützenkompanie*) had three rifle platoons, and each 50-strong rifle platoon (*Schützenzug*) was composed of a platoon staff, a light-grenade-launcher team and four rifle sections, each section (*Schützengruppe*) having ten men.

All units of a motorised division (*Infanteriedivision(mot.)*) were armoured or motorised, and in early 1940 motorised divisions were reduced to two motorised regiments, giving a divisional total of 14,319 men. A mountain division (*Gebirgsdivision*) had 14,131 men with two 6,506-strong mountain regiments, plus support units and services, all with mountain capability.

A 14,373-strong armoured division (*Panzerdivision*) had an armoured brigade (two regiments of 1,700 men divided into two battalions) and a 4,409-strong motorised rifle brigade (rifle regiment and motorcycle battalion), the remaining support units and the services being armoured or motorised.

A 10-11,000-strong light division (*Leichte Division*) had between one and four 638-strong armoured battalions and one or two 2,295-strong motorised cavalry regiments, before reorganising as Panzer Divisions 6-9 in October 1939–January 1940. The 16,000-strong 1 Cavalry Division (*1.Kavalleriedivision*) had four 1,440-strong mounted (*Reiter*) regiments (each with two mounted battalions), a cavalry (*Kavallerie*) regiment (one mounted, one bicycle battalion) and a bicycle battalion, other support units and services being mounted or motorised.

Guerian on the day of his promotion to General der Panzertruppen and his appointment as Commander of Mobile Troops, 20 November 1938. He is wearing the M1935 officers' service uniform with a particularly good example of the M1935 peaked cap. Note the First World War bravery and Wehrmacht long-service awards. (Brian Davis Collection)

15 March 1939. Reconnaissance troops in field uniform, wearing the regulation M1934 rubberised greatcoats, ride a BMW R12 745cc motorcycle combination through the streets of the conquered city of Prague. They carry minimal field equipment appropriate for this unopposed invasion. Note the dejected appearance of the local citizens. (Brian Davis Collection)

In 1937 Germany was divided into 13 military districts, numbered I–XIII, and from 1939 these were the bases of the Replacement Army. The depots, schools and training units of a *Wehrkreis* (district), manned and equipped initially one, and later as many as five, corps, for the Field Army, keeping them supplied with a continuous stream of reinforcements. As Germany expanded its territory at its neighbours' expense to form *Großdeutschland* (Greater Germany) the existing districts were expanded and six new ones formed from August 1938–October 1942. They provided conscripts for the war-effort, many of whom were not ethnic Germans or even sympathetic to the German cause.

THE STRATEGY

German strategy combined two concepts: the traditional 'Decisive Manoeuvre', developed by Prussian General von Moltke in the 1850s, and the 'Armoured Concept', usually known as *Blitzkrieg*, proposed by Heinz Guderian in the late 1920s. Both required rapidly mobilised forces to attack on consecutive fronts, mounting a concentrated surprise attack on one front, defeating the enemy in a few days or weeks, before regrouping to attack on the second front, thus avoiding a costly defensive two-front war which Germany would inevitably lose.

'Decisive Manoeuvre', used infantry to attack the enemy's line of retreat, trapping it in pockets. Blitzkrieg, however used concentrations of tanks, mechanised infantry and Luftwaffe dive-bombers to punch a hole in the enemy line, and penetrate into rear areas to destroy the enemy command centre, forcing a total collapse in enemy morale. The Polish and Scandinavian campaigns were conducted according to the principles of 'Decisive Manoeuvre', while the Western Offensive was Blitzkrieg.

Both strategies demanded that Germany be the aggressor, a position in line with the Third Reich's xenophobic and expansionist ideology. Germany had the vital advantages of surprise and of choosing the time, place and conditions of the battles. Its opponents pinned their hopes on neutrality, diplomatic skills and static frontier defences. They were psychologically unwilling to fight, and reluctant to prepare for war.

The Flower Wars

Hitler's political manoeuvrings, and Franco-British reluctance to risk war, gave the German Army five bloodless victories before September 1939. Hitler's troops annexed neighbouring territories in operations known as the *Blumenkriege*, or Flower Wars, a reference to the flowers often thrown by local ethnic Germans to welcome German forces.

On 7 March 1936 30,000 troops from the 5th, 9th, 15th and 16th Infantry Divisions marched across the Rhine and occupied the demilitarised Saar region on the west bank. On 12 March 1938 200,000 troops of the 8th Army (VII and XIII Corps, and 2.Panzerdivision) invaded Austria, annexing it, dividing it into *Wehrkreise* XVII and XVIII in April 1938, and absorbing the Austrian Army as 44th and 45th Infantry, 4th Light and 2nd and 3rd Mountain Divisions.

The Army had originally expected to deploy 39 divisions in five armies (numbers 2,8,10,12,14) against Czechoslovakia in 'Operation

An Oberst im Generalstab relaxes in his garden. He is wearing undress uniform with Kolben collar-patches and M1935 adjutants' aiguillettes for General Staff officers, the M1935 field tunic and the M1938 field cap. Germany, 1939. (Brian Davis Collection)

Troops of the Artillery Instruction Regiment in Jütebog, responsible for training artillery officer cadets in Germany, 1939. Wearing the M1935 field uniform, they demonstrate firing a 3.7cm Pak 35/36 L/45 anti-tank gun. Note the Karabiner 98k rifles and the minimal field equipment – M1931 canvas bread-bags and M1938 gas mask canisters, but no Y-straps. (Brian Davis Collection)

Green', but following the Munich Agreement in September 1938, it occupied the Sudetenland border areas without bloodshed from 1 to 10 October 1938 with elements of the five neighbouring German corps – IV, VII, VIII, XIII, XVII, XVIII. The Sudetenland was incorporated into *Wehrkreise* IV, VII, VIII, XIII and XVII. On 15 March 1939 these units occupied the rest of Bohemia-Moravia, designated *Wehrkreis Böhmen und Mähren* in October 1942. Finally, on 23 March 1939 elements of I Corps annexed the Memel district of Western Lithuania to *Wehrkreis I*.

The 600-man volunteer *Gruppe Imker*, consisting of the Panzergruppe *Drohne* armoured unit with two signals companies and anti-tank, supply and repair elements, saw limited combat in the Spanish Civil War from July 1936 to May 1939 as part of the Luftwaffe's Condor Legion.

The Polish campaign and the Phoney War

On 26 August 1939 the Wehrmacht began a secret partial mobilisation for 'Operation White', the invasion of Poland, leading to full mobilisation on 3 September. On 1 September the army attacked, joining up with *Bau-Lehr Bataillon zbV 800* commandos and other Army Intelligence (*Abwehr*) units who had already infiltrated the region to secure vital bridges.

The invasion force, consisting of 1,512,000 men, was organised in two army groups totalling 53 divisions (37 infantry, four motorised, three mountain, three light, six Panzer). It attacked on three fronts. Army Group *Nord*, under Generaloberst Fedor von Bock with 3rd and 4th Armies, attacked from north-east Germany and East Prussia. *Süd*, commanded by Generaloberst Gerd von Rundstedt with 8th, 10th and 14th Armies, advanced from south-east Germany and northern Slovakia, supported by 1st and 2nd Slovak divisions. The 1,100,000-strong Polish Army, organised in 40 infantry divisions, two mechanised and 11 mounted cavalry brigades, and deployed too close to the German frontier, was already being outflanked when, on 17 September, seven armies (41 divisions and equivalents) of the Soviet Red Army attacked them in the rear. Threatened on four fronts, the heavily outnumbered Polish Army officially surrendered on 27 September, and had ceased all hostilities on 6 October. Occupied Poland came under military control – Ciechanòw and Suwalki districts were incorporated in *Wehrkreis* I in September 1939, Bialystok in August 1941; Danzig and north-west Poland as XX and western Poland as XXI in September 1939; and south-east Poland as *General-Gouvernement* in September 1942.

During the eight-month 'Phoney War', Anglo-French forces massed on the western German frontier, briefly occupying the Saar District in September 1939, giving the Wehrmacht a free hand in Poland and Scandinavia, and allowing it to choose the conditions of the Western Offensive in May 1940.

Denmark and Norway

Anxious that the Anglo-French forces might attack Germany through Norway and Denmark, Hitler decided to invade these militarily weak neutral states in a pre-emptive strike called 'Operation Weserübung', commanded by General der Infanterie Nikolaus von Falkenhorst.

On 9 April 1940 *Höheres Kommando z.b.V. XXXI* (XXXI Special Corps), with the 170th and 198th Infantry Divisions, 11th Motorised Rifle Brigade and 40th Special Panzer Battalion, attacked Denmark. The inexperienced Danish Army, with 6,600 troops organised in two infantry divisions, its strategic position hopeless, was forced to surrender after four hours' limited resistance.

On the same day XXI Corps, with 3rd Mountain, 69th and 163rd Infantry Divisions, disembarked in Norway, later reinforced by 2nd

A signalman of the Signal Instruction Battalion in Halle, Germany 1939, responsible for training artillery officer cadets. He wears standard M1935 field uniform and, for the purposes of the gas exercise, a M1938 gas mask, whilst operating a M1933 field telephone. His unit letter is shown on his M1933 pointed shoulder-straps without piping. (Brian Davis Collection)

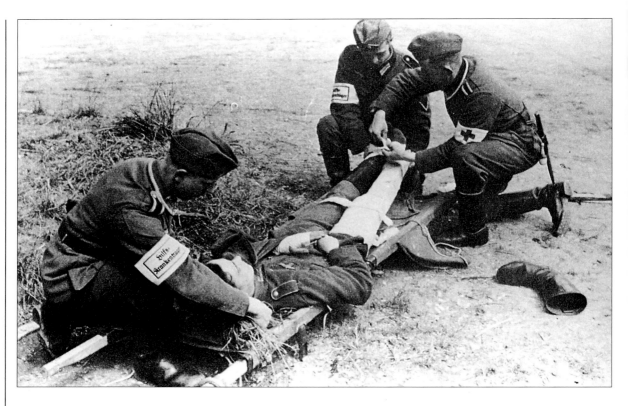

Mountain, 181st, 196th and 214th Infantry Divisions, with 40th Special Panzer Battalion providing token armour. They totalled some 100,000 men. They engaged six infantry divisions of the Norwegian Army, (with only 25,000 of its 90,000 men mobilised), backed up by the Allied Expeditionary Force with the equivalent of two infantry divisions, and forced an Allied evacuation and a Norwegian surrender on 9 June 1940.

The Low Countries

For 'Operation Yellow', the Western Offensive, the German Army assembled 2,750,000 men in 91 divisions, divided among three army groups. 'A' under Generaloberst von Rundstedt with 4th, 12th and 16th Armies, including Panzergruppe *von Kleist*, was to advance through Belgium into France. 'B' commanded by Generaloberst von Bock with 6th and 18th Armies, would attack the Netherlands and Belgium, whilst 'C' under Generaloberst Wilhelm Ritter von Leeb, with 1st and 7th Armies, would pin down French forces on the Maginot Line. These forces totalled 75 infantry divisions (including 22nd Airlanding Division), one Luftwaffe airborne division, four motorised, one mountain, one cavalry and ten Panzer divisions, with a further 42 divisions in reserve.

The offensive began on 10 May 1940, with commandos and *Abwehr* already active in the Netherlands and Belgium. Army Group B's 18th Army, with nine divisions plus airportable and parachute troops, attacked the neutral Netherlands, rapidly overwhelming the inexperienced Dutch Army. With 250,000 men organised in ten poorly trained infantry divisions, the Dutch put up an unexpectedly spirited defence, but surrendered on 15 May following the bombing of Rotterdam.

Germany, 1939. A Sanitätsunteroffizier in M1935 undress uniform with the M1935 other ranks' field cap and Medical Corps red-cross arm-band, instructs in first-aid infantry stretcher-bearers, who wear black on white *Hilfskrankenträger* armbands. (Brian Davis Collection)

Luxembourg fell on 10 May to 16th Army, its 82-man 'Volunteer Company' offering only token resistance. The same day Army Group A, joined by 6th Army from Army Group B, began its advance through neutral Belgium, spearheaded by an airborne attack on Fort Eben-Emael. The 600,000-strong Belgian Army, organised in 18 infantry, two mountain and two cavalry divisions, supported by British and French troops, initially resisted strongly. Its morale declined as it retreated before the relentless German advance, led by the powerful Panzergruppe *von Kleist*'s surprise outflanking attack through the supposedly impenetrable Ardennes hill country. On 28 May the Belgian Army surrendered.

The Battle of France

On 16 May Army Groups A and B began to advance into France. They were confronted by the 4,320,000-strong French Army, organised in Army Groups 1-3, with eight armies composed of 38 infantry, one fortress, nine motorised, three light mechanised, four light cavalry, and three armoured divisions, a total of 87 divisions, supported by nine British, one Czechoslovak and four Polish infantry divisions.

Two NCOs in undress uniform with M1935 field greatcoats having field rations in Germany, September 1939. Note the NCOs' sword-knot attached to the bayonet of the Feldwebel (right), the absence of shoulder-strap numbers, and the regulation mess-tins. (ECPA)

A force of nine Panzer divisions, comprising Panzergruppe *von Kleist*, XV Corps and General der Panzertruppen Heinz Guderian's XIX Corps (redesignated Panzergruppe *Guderian* on 1 June) with the *Großdeutschland* Motorised Regiment, burst through the French 1st Army Group at Sedan, reaching the Channel coast on 22 May. Concerned that the unit, containing almost all Germany's armoured troops, had outrun its logistical tail and supporting infantry, and was vulnerable to an Allied counterattack, Von Rundstedt ordered a halt on 23 May, allowing the Allies to evacuate 338,226 British, French and Belgian troops from Dunkirk from 27 May to 4 June.

On 5 June Army 'Operation Red' commenced. Army Group B advanced along the French Channel and Atlantic coasts, stopping before Bordeaux on 22 June, while A headed through central France and C forced the Maginot Line. The French Army signed an armistice on 25 June. Eupen and Malmédy districts in Belgium were annexed and joined *Wehrkreis* VI, Luxembourg and Lorraine *Wehrkreis* XII, and Alsace Wehrkreis V. Northern, western and eastern France was occupied, leaving central and southern France unoccupied as a nominally independent French state under Field Marshal Pétain.

The verdict on Blitzkrieg

The Blitzkrieg period had restored the reputation of the German armed forces, but weaknesses had emerged. Success had confirmed Hitler's belief in his own genius and the corresponding inferiority of his professional generals. Jealousy between the *OKW*, the Wehrmacht High Command, and the

Poland, September 1939. Dispatch riders in field uniform. They wear M1934 rubberised greatcoats, with shoulder-straps removed for security, and M1935 dispatch-cases. Their M1916 helmets were already obsolete but were still widely encountered in the early years of the war. (Brian Davis Collection)

OKH, the Army High Command, exacerbated by the fact that Hitler controlled both, led to a division of authority. The Danish and Norwegian campaigns were controlled by *OKW*, and the Polish and Western campaigns by *OKH*. Panzergruppe *Kleist*'s classic Blitzkrieg tactics had proved brilliantly successful, but the infantry performance in Norway had been less decisive. Finally, the swift advances of the Blitzkrieg had enabled large numbers of enemy troops to evade capture and organise themselves as guerrilla armies, a constant threat to the German occupation authorities.

The Armies of Occupation

The Army established transit prisoner-of-war camps (*Dulags*) in occupied territory which collected enemy POWs before transfer to the officer camps (*Oflags*) and other-rank camps (*Stalags*). They were organised by each *Wehrkreis* and guarded by *Landesschützen* units unfit for front-line combat.

Occupied territories were placed under military governments – Poland under the *General-Gouvernement* (until September 1942); Denmark (from August 1943); Belgium-Northern France. The rest of occupied France was organised under *Militärbefehlshaber* (Army Governors), and Netherlands and Norway under *Wehrmacht-befehlshaber* (Armed Forces Governors). Each governor controlled regimental-level district commands (*Oberfeldkommandanture*), which in turn were subdivided into battalion-level sub-districts (*Feldkommandanture*) and then into smaller metropolitan, urban or rural commands.

In addition three conquered territories had occupation armies. Norway, from December 1940, had 'Norway Army' (*Armee Norwegen*) made up of three, sometimes four Corps. The Netherlands, from June 1942, had LXXXVIII Corps. Army Groups A, B and C remained in Occupied France, to be replaced in October 1940 by Army Group D with 1st, 7th and 15th Armies.

TABLE 1 GERMAN ARMY ORDERS OF DRESS 1 SEPTEMBER 1939 – 9 MAY 1945

Order of Dress	General-officers, Infantry officers and bandmaster officers	Technical non-commissioned officers, Infantry senior and junior non-commissioned officers and men	When worn
Großer Gesellschaftsanzug Formal ceremonial uniform	Service cap; dress tunic & medals/piped field tunic & ribbons; aiguillettes; trousers & shoes; white gloves; sword; knot.	—	Presenting reports; receptions; theatre; concerts.
Kleiner Gesellschaftsanzug Informal ceremonial uniform	Service cap; dress tunic/piped field tunic; ribbons; trousers & shoes; white gloves; sword; knot.	—	Presenting reports; receptions; church-parades; funerals; theatre; concerts.
Paradeanzug Parade uniform	Helmet/peaked cap; dress tunic; medals; aiguillettes; dress greatcoat; belt; breeches & riding-boots; grey gloves; sword; knot.	Helmet; dress tunic/field tunic; medals; dress greatcoat; marksman's lanyard; belt, piped/plain trousers, marching boots; grey gloves (NCOs); sword, knot (TNCOs, SNCOs); Y-straps, ammo-pouches, rifle, bayonet, knot (JNCOs, men).	Parades; church-parades; funerals.
Ausgehanzug Walking out uniform	Service cap; dress tunic/piped field tunic; ribbons; dress greatcoat; trousers & shoes; white gloves; sword; knot.	Service cap; dress tunic/field tunic; ribbons; dress greatcoat; marksman's lanyard; belt; piped/plain trousers, shoes; grey gloves (NCOs); sword, knot (TNCOs, SNCOs); bayonet, knot (JNCOs, men).	Walking-out; church-parades; funerals.
Meldeanzug Reporting uniform	Service cap; dress tunic/piped field tunic; ribbons; belt; breeches & riding boots; grey gloves; sword; knot.	Service cap; field tunic; ribbons; marksman's lanyard; belt; plain trousers, marching-boots; grey gloves (NCOs); sword, knot (TNCOs, SNCOs); bayonet, knot (JNCOs, men).	Presenting reports.
Dienstanzug Service uniform	Service cap; field tunic; ribbons; field greatcoat; belt; breeches & riding-boots; grey gloves; pistol; holster.	Service cap (TNCOs, SNCOs); helmet/field cap (JNCOs, men); field-tunic; ribbons; field greatcoat; belt, plain trousers, marching boots; grey gloves (NCOs); pistol, holster (TNCOs, SNCOs); Y-straps, ammo-pouches; rifle, bayonet, knot (JNCOs, men).	Manoeuvres; inspections; church-parades; funerals; courts martial; parades.
Kleiner Dienstanzug Undress uniform	Service cap; dress tunic/field tunic; ribbons; field greatcoat; breeches & riding boots/ trousers & shoes; grey gloves; pistol; holster.	Service cap/field cap; field tunic; ribbons; field greatcoat; belt; plain trousers, marching-boots; grey gloves (NCOs); pistol, holster (TNCOs, SNCOs); y-straps, ammo-pouches; rifle, bayonet, knot (JNCOs, men).	Manoeuvres; inspections; rifle-ranges; instructional classes; barracks-yards; presenting reports (officers).
Wachanzug Guard uniform	Helmet/field-cap; field tunic (dress tunic for guards of honour); ribbons; field greatcoat; belt; breeches & riding-boots; grey gloves; pistol; holster.	Helmet/field cap; field tunic; ribbons; field greatcoat; marksman's lanyard; belt; plain/piped trousers, marching boots; grey gloves (NCOs); pistol, holster (TNCOs, SNCOs); Y-straps, ammo-pouches; rifle, bayonet, knot (JNCOs, men).	Standing guard.
Feldanzug Field uniform	Helmet/field cap; field tunic; ribbons; field greatcoat; belt; breeches & riding-boots; grey gloves; equipment (not general-officers); pistol; holster.	Helmet/field cap; field tunic; ribbons; field greatcoat; belt, plain trousers, marching-boots; grey gloves (NCOs); pistol, holster (TNCOs, SNCOs); field-equipment; rifle, bayonet (JNCOs, men).	Manoeuvres; combat.
Arbeitsanzug Fatigue uniform	—	Field cap; fatigue tunic; belt; fatigue trousers, marching-boots.	Fatigue duties.

THE UNIFORM OF THE GERMAN ARMY

All dates connected with the introduction of new uniforms, equipment and insignia give the date of the Army Order. However, as in all armies, there was a delay (ranging from a few weeks to as much as two years) in new items reaching individual units, especially front-line units, remote garrisons, or in the Replacement Army. Furthermore, individual soldiers,

13

especially senior officers, often preferred to retain obsolete items if they were of sentimental value, or of better quality than the replacement. They gave the owner an air of individuality and marked him as an experienced 'old sweat'. An army order of 10 July 1942 decreed that all obsolete clothing could continue to be worn for the duration of the war.

The most visible symbol of the Wehrmacht was the breast eagle, the *Hoheitsabzeichen*, or 'Sovereignty Badge', worn by all ranks above the right breast pocket of most uniform items, and identifying the wearer as fit to bear arms. The Army version, introduced 17 February 1934, with effect from 1 May 1934, depicted an eagle with straight, outstretched wings grasping a circled swastika. Most other uniformed organisations, including the Waffen-SS, introduced various styles of eagle badges, but were obliged to wear them on the left upper arm, since the right breast was reserved for the Wehrmacht (and, curiously enough, the National Socialist Flying Corps, the NSFK).

The various uniform items of the new Army uniform began to appear following publication of the Dress Regulations of 8 April 1935. These uniforms and insignia were developments of, and continued the traditions of, the Army's four predecessors – the *Reichsheer* (National Army) of the Second Reich (18 January 1871–11 November 1918); the *Friedensheer* (Peacetime Army, 11 November 1918–5 March 1919); the *Vorläufige Reichswehr* (Temporary National Armed Forces, 6 March 1919–31 December 1920); and, most importantly, the *Reichsheer* (usually, but incorrectly, known as the *Reichswehr*) of the German Republic (1 January 1921–15 March 1935).

By the end of 1935 the main uniform styles were established. The basic uniform colour was a greenish-grey, introduced 2 July 1929 and given the traditional but inaccurate title of *feldgrau*, 'field grey' (originally designating a plain mid-grey introduced 23 February 1910).

An Unterfeldwebel (left), acting as section leader, in field uniform orders his infantry section to attack. He is wearing standard M1935 field uniform with M1935 helmet with a rubber band for securing camouflage, and minimal equipment – 6 x 30 issue binoculars and the M1931 canvas bread-bag. The deputy section leader (right), laden with 6 x 30 binoculars, M1935 map-case, M1938 gas mask canister and M1931 camouflage shelter-quarter, observes the enemy in Poland, September 1939. (Brian Davis Collection)

Facings were in a bluish dark-green 'facing-cloth', finely woven to give an appearance of a thin felt, introduced 29 June 1935, and the same material was usually used for branch colour patches and pipings. *Reichswehr* uniform items, in M1929 *feldgrau* but with a darker greenish-grey facing-cloth, should have been withdrawn by 1937, but were still occasionally encountered in the 1939/40 period.

The Regulations of April 1935 prescribed ten orders of dress in peacetime for officers, two ceremonial uniforms and a parade uniform for formal occasions; a walking-out and reporting uniform for semi-formal occasions; service, undress and guard uniforms for training and barracks duties; the field uniform for combat; and sports dress (omitted in this study). (See Table 1 for more details.) Non-commissioned officers and other ranks had nine, omitting the ceremonial uniforms and adding a fatigue uniform for work-duties in barracks or in the field. Some uniform items were manufactured in different versions for officers and other ranks, while others were standard items worn by all ranks.

New regulations were issued on 28 December 1939 to cover the wartime period and the earlier strict observance of regulations eased. The types of uniforms were simplified. Service uniform could be worn on most formal and semi-formal occasions, but, inevitably, the field uniform became the most common uniform encountered in the front line and rear areas. Furthermore, Replacement Army units were often issued captured Austrian, Czech, Dutch, French, and even British uniform items, dyed and remodelled to conform to German patterns.

Officers' ceremonial uniform

The full ceremonial uniform consisted of the M1935 officers' peaked service cap, dress tunic (*Waffenrock*) with medals, aiguillettes and trousers, standard black lace-up shoes, officers' white suede gloves, and sabre. The informal ceremonial uniform omitted the aiguillettes, and substituted ribbons for medals.

Assault engineers in M1935 field uniform prepare to advance in Poland, September 1939. The sapper (left) carries the short model wire-cutters in a black leather case on his left back hip, also the M1938 gas mask canister, M1931 camouflage shelter-quarter, M1931 canvas bread-bag and M1931 canteen. His companion's bayonet and folded entrenching tool are prominently displayed. (Brian Davis Collection)

The saddle-shaped **officers' peaked cap**, introduced 10 September 1935 and worn with most officers' uniforms, had a high crown at the front falling steeply to the sides. Later caricatured as typically German, it was in fact a revolutionary design, replacing the traditional 'plate' style with its high cap-band and low circular crown. It was manufactured in *feldgrau* tricot or 'eskimo' material. The M1935 eagle and swastika badge, manufactured in bright aluminium, was worn above a stamped bright aluminium red (inner)-white-black (outer) national cockade in an oak-leaf wreath, on the bluish dark-green facing-cloth cap band. There was 2mm thick piping around the crown in branch-of-service colour, and above and below the cap band, a plain black-lacquered vulcanised fibre peak, and a matt aluminium wire chin-cord secured by two 12mm bright aluminium pebbled buttons. General-officers had gold-coloured metallic woven cord cap-pipings and gold wire; from 15 July 1938 this became yellow artificial 'celleon' wire, woven chin-cords with matt gold pebbled buttons. Hand-embroidered bright silver or bright aluminium bullion badges on a bluish dark-green facing-cloth backing were per-mitted on fine-cloth privately purchased caps.

The style, though not the colour, of the *feldgrau* tricot pocketless waisted **officers' dress-tunic**, adopted 29 June 1935, invoked the proud military traditions of the *Reichsheer* of the German Empire. It had bluish dark-green facing-cloth collars and cuffs, branch colour facing-cloth pipings, and bright aluminium pebbled buttons and wire braids. The piped front was secured by eight buttons, with three on each of the piped ornamental back 'tail-pockets'. Insignia consisted of the officers' superior dress-quality breast-eagle, collar-patches, cuff-patches and shoulder boards. The bright, hand-embroidered, flat aluminium bullion breast eagle had a bluish dark-green backing. The piped collar had M1935 branch colour facing-cloth collar-patches, with two bright aluminium wire embroidered 'Guards' braids' developed from those worn by élite Guards regiments of the Imperial *Reichsheer*. Similarly, the piped cuffs had two branch colour cuff-patches, each with a button and braid. For shoulder-boards see Table 3. Privately purchased tunics were usually shaped at the waist and had higher, stiffer collars.

General-officers had a bright gold bullion or golden-yellow hand-embroidered thread breast-eagle on a bluish dark-green facing-cloth backing. The collar and cuff-patches showed the bright gold bullion or 'celleon' hand-embroidered thread *Alt-Larisch* design introduced 22 March 1900. After 1939 they were in matt yellow yarn picked out in dark yellow or buff, on a bright-red facing-cloth patch.

On 21 March 1940 further manufacture of the *Waffenrock* was forbidden, and existing tunics were to be converted to field tunics by removing the facing-cloth cuffs and tail pockets and substituting field-quality insignia. In future only the **officers' 'piped field tunic'**, introduced 12 July 1937 as an alternative to the *Waffenrock*, would be worn in full-dress. This was a field tunic with

An infantryman in Poland in October 1939 wearing the M1935 field uniform, with reversed shoulder-straps to conceal unit insignia, searches a Polish prisoner. There is a particularly good view of his improvised assault-pack, consisting of a bayonet strapped to his entrenching-tool, with the M1931 camouflage shelter-quarter and the M1931 mess-kit tied to his belt with belt supporting-straps. (ECPA)

Poland, 18 September 1939. German officers in M1935 field uniform relax during negotiations with a Soviet Red Army officer (centre, in a greatcoat, carrying a map-case) over arrangements for partitioning defeated Poland between Germany and the Soviet Union. Note the German guard, in M1935 field uniform with field greatcoat, presenting arms. (Josef Charita)

branch colour collar facings, front and cuff pipings, and dress-quality collar-patches, shoulder-boards and breast-eagles. The M1920 service-tunic (introduced 22 December 1920) or the M1928 service-tunic (introduced 31 October 1928), with respectively eight or six buttons, diagonally flapped concealed hip-pockets and branch colour facing-cloth front piping, was often retained, especially by general-officers.

The standard stone-grey trousers had a 2mm branch colour piping down the outer seam, flanked on each side by a 4cm branch colour stripe for general-officers. The bright aluminium wire dress aiguillette (gold, later 'celleon' for general-officers) was introduced 29 June 1935.

Officers' formal and semi-formal uniforms

The parade uniform consisted of the standard M1935 steel helmet or officers' peaked cap; the officers' *Waffenrock* with aiguillettes, M1937 officers' dress belt; breeches with black leather riding-boots and spurs, grey gloves and sword. The officers' M1935 dress greatcoat could also be worn, if ordered.

The standard M1935 **steel helmet** was introduced 25 June 1935, a development of the M1916 and M1918 helmets, with their prominent side-lugs. Painted matt *feldgrau* a black-white-red diagonally striped aluminium national shield was fixed to the right side, and a silver-white Wehrmacht eagle on a black painted aluminium shield on the left side, as ordered on 17 February 1934. Officers could also wear lightweight aluminium *Vulkanfiber* helmets on parade.

The **officers' dress belt**, introduced 9 July 1937, was made of bright aluminium brocade with two 5cm bluish dark-green stripes. The circular buckle was stamped bright aluminium (gold-plated or galvanically gilded for general-officers) showing a Wehrmacht eagle with folded wings in a wreath. The stone-grey officers' riding-breeches were plain, general-officers retaining their pipings and broad stripes.

The superior-quality officers' *feldgrau* **dress greatcoat**, introduced 10 September 1935, had a bluish dark-green facing-cloth collar and two rows of six matt *feldgrau* buttons, a back half-belt secured by two buttons, dress-quality shoulder-boards and the back seam sewn up. General-

General der Artillerie Halder, Chief of General Staff (left) and Generaloberst von Brauchitsch, Chief of the Army High Command (right), photographed in Germany, 4 October 1939, discussing strategy in Poland. Both wear M1935 undress uniform. Halder wears a remodelled M1929 service tunic, with an impressive array of First World War and Wehrmacht long-service medal ribbons, while von Brauchitsch, in a M1935 field tunic, has only the Nazi Party badge and the 1939 Iron Cross First Class. (Brian Davis Collection)

officers had matt gold pebbled buttons, leaving the top two buttons open to show bright-red facing-cloth lapel-linings. From 14 May 1937 all officers wearing collar decorations were also permitted to leave these buttons open. General-officers also wore the leather greatcoat with plain lapel-linings

'Walking-out' uniform consisted of the officers' service-cap, standard dress-tunic or officers' piped field tunic with ribbons, dress greatcoat if ordered, long trousers, lace-up shoes, white gloves and sword. The 'reporting uniform' added the M1934 belt, breeches and riding-boots, and grey gloves. The dark-brown **leather officers' belt** and cross-strap, introduced 18 May 1934, had a pebbled matt aluminium open-claw rectangular buckle, which was matt gilt for generals. On 20 November 1939 the cross-strap was abolished.

Officers' training and barracks uniforms

Service uniform consisted of the officers' peaked cap, M1933 field tunic with ribbons, M1935 field greatcoat, leather-belt, breeches and riding-boots, grey suede gloves, standard pistol and holster.

The officers' **field tunic** was introduced 5 May 1933, replacing the M1920 *Reichswehr* service-tunic. It was manufactured from superior quality *feldgrau* cloth with five matt-grey painted pebbled buttons, four patch pockets, turn-back cuffs and a *feldgrau* cloth collar, replaced by *feldgrau* facing-cloth on 26 July 1934 and by bluish dark-green facing-cloth in March 1936. All insignia was field-quality: the breast-eagle was in matt aluminium thread on a bluish dark-green facing-cloth backing; the bluish dark-green facing-cloth collar-patches had two matt aluminium

An Oberfeldwebel in M1935 field uniform wearing the M1935 steel helmet, displaying the M1934 Wehrmacht eagle. The M1938 collar-patches and the obsolete M1935 field shoulder-straps do not show branch insignia and he has removed his white metal unit insignia for security reasons. Note the company number (1 Company, 1 Battalion), worn by NCOs and enlisted men on the shoulder-strap button, replaced from September 1939 by a plain pebbled button. Germany, January 1940. (Brian Davis Collection)

'Guards' braids', each with a branch colour silk-embroidered centre cord. For shoulder-boards see Table 3. Many general-officers retained the M1920 or M1928 service tunic with field-quality insignia and no front piping.

The **officers' field greatcoat** was like the dress greatcoat, but with field-quality shoulder-boards and the back seam left open.

In the 'undress' uniform, officers omitted the belt and could wear standard piped long trousers and lace-up shoes. With the 'Guard' uniform they wore the helmet, the M1934 or M1938 field cap; the field tunic or, if leading a Guard of Honour, the dress tunic; field greatcoat; brown belt; breeches and riding-boots, grey suede gloves, and a pistol and holster.

The M1934 **officers' 'old-style' field cap**, introduced 24 March 1934, became the M1935 peaked cap with the addition of a bluish dark-green cap band on 10 September 1935, and the omission of the metal crown stiffener, chincords and buttons. The visor was made of soft black patent leather and, from 30 October 1935, the eagle, cockade and wreath were of bright aluminium thread on a bluish dark-green backing.

The visorless flapped M1938 **officers' 'new-style' field cap**, introduced 6 December 1938, was made of *feldgrau* cloth, piped along the crown and the front of the flap with 3mm aluminium thread cord. The narrow aluminium cord national cockade was enclosed by a branch colour chevron, point up, in facing-cloth, with a machine-woven or hand-embroidered bright aluminium thread eagle on a bluish dark-green backing above. From 24 October 1939 general-officers wore gold thread crown and flap piping and a gold artificial silk chevron.

Officers' field uniform

In the field all Army officers except platoon leaders wore the standard steel helmet, officers' field tunic, with the field greatcoat if ordered, brown belt, breeches and riding-boots and grey suede gloves. Personal

NCOs of the Army Patrol Service in M1935 service uniform, with other ranks' M1935 field greatcoats and M1935 field caps, parade for duty in a German garrison town in 1940. The obsolete M1920 adjutants' aiguillettes on their right shoulder constitute their badges of office. (ECPA)

Germany, April 1940. A private of a newly created War Correspondents' Company in M1935 undress uniform with an M1935 field cap, takes a trip on the Rhine. He wears the lemon-yellow Signals branch colour on his shoulder-straps and cap, as well as the newly introduced *Propagandakompanie* sleeve-title. (F. Herrmann)

field equipment was usually limited to the P08 Luger or P-38 Walther pistol in a smooth leather holster – general-officers and field officers favoured the smaller Walther 7.65mm PPK – and 6x30 black binoculars in a smooth black or tan leather or bakelite case carried on the right front hip. Behind the front line the M1934 or M1938 field caps replaced the helmet.

In the field the shape and colour of the helmet was often camouflaged by daubing it with mud, or tying chicken-wire or the straps of the M1931 bread-bag and securing foliage to them. On 21 March 1940 the conspicuous national shield was removed and the helmet surface roughened and repainted from matt *feldgrau* to matt slate-grey.

From 31 October 1939 all officers below general-officer in combat units were ordered to wear the M1935 other ranks' field tunic, trousers and marching-boots with the black leather belt and officers' field-quality shoulder-boards. Many officers, however, continued to wear their former uniforms or modified the other ranks' tunic by adding officers' roll-back cuffs, collar-patches and the sharper-pointed, higher officers' collars.

Subalterns acting as infantry platoon leaders wore the standard **riflemen's field equipment** adding the brown or black leather M1935 dispatch-case on the left front hip, binoculars, compass and signal-whistle. Riflemen's field equipment consisted of the standard smooth or grained black leather M1939 infantry support Y-straps with aluminium fittings (introduced 18 April 1939), supporting two sets of three black leather ammunition pouches for the rifle. The bayonet in a black scabbard with the black leather cavalry bayonet-frog (introduced 25 January

An Oberstleutnant of Panzer troops on the Belgian frontier, May 1940. He wears the M1935 black tank-crew uniform with M1940 officers' field cap, wearing the 1914 Iron Cross 2nd Class ribbon with 1939 bar in his button-hole. He is talking to a colleague, who is wearing the M1935 officers' peaked cap with Panzer pink *waffenfarbe* (branch-colour facing-cloth piping). (Josef Charita)

1939) and entrenching-tool were worn on the left back hip. On the right back hip, the M1931 *feldgrau* canvas bread-bag and M1931 brown felt-covered canteen and black painted aluminium cup. Webbing supported the M1931 mess-kit and M1931 camouflage shelter-quarter on the upper back, and on the lower back the M1930 or M1938 gas mask in the distinctive *feldgrau*-painted cylindrical corrugated metal canister. The dark greenish-brown gas cape hung on the chest from a thin brown leather strap and a field flashlight was usually carried on the left shoulder. By September 1939 most officers had the MP38 submachine gun, for which two olive-green canvas M1938 magazine pouches were issued to replace the black leather ammunition-pouches.

Other ranks' parade uniform

Parade Uniform for other ranks consisted of the standard M1935 steel helmet; the OR M1935 *Waffenrock* or M1933 field tunic with medals, and, if ordered, the OR M1935 dress greatcoat; standard M1935 piped or plain trousers and marching-boots; the M1936 marksman's lanyard, M1935 belt, bayonet and bayonet-frog. All NCOs wore grey suede gloves. Technical and senior NCOs carried a sword, while junior NCOs and men wore standard M1939 Y-straps, M1908 ammunition-pouches and carried a rifle.

The other ranks' **Waffenrock**, adopted 29 June 1935, was identical to the officers' pattern with bright aluminium pebbled buttons, but made of fine quality (rather than superior) *feldgrau* cloth, with other ranks' dress insignia. The collar had M1935 branch colour facings, collar-patches with two bright aluminium thread 'Guards braids'. The cuffs had two branch colour badge-cloth cuff-patches, each with a bright aluminium pebbled button on a bright aluminium thread braid. The matt silver-grey machine-woven breast eagle had a bluish dark-green facing-cloth backing. The bluish dark-green facing-cloth shoulder-straps had rounded ends and a branch colour piping around the outer edge. For

The crew of an army light anti-aircraft unit on the alert for Allied aircraft in France, May 1940. The crewmen are wearing the typically soiled M1933 drill fatigue-uniform to avoid soiling their field uniforms. (Josef Charita)

shoulder-strap and sleeve rank insignia see Table 3. NCOs wore 1.5cm wide bright aluminium 'double-diamond' pattern yarn braid introduced 10 September 1935 on the front and top edge of the stand-up collar and on the top and back edge of the cuff to indicate their status. Privately-purchased tunics could be made of officers' tricot cloth with higher collars and tighter waisting.

The **other ranks' field tunic** in *feldgrau* cloth with matt-grey painted pebbled buttons was introduced on 5 May 1933 with the colour of the collar changing from *feldgrau* facing-cloth to bluish dark-green facing-cloth 10 September 1935. It resembled the officers' tunic, but the skirt was longer and cuffs were without the turn-backs. Insignia was of other ranks' field-quality.

The bluish dark-green facing-cloth M1935 collar-patches, introduced 10 September 1935, had two *feldgrau* braid 'Guards braids' each with branch colour facing-cloth centre stripes. They were replaced on 26 November 1938 by the 'standard braid', bluish dark-green facing-cloth stripes so the collar-patches no longer indicated branch affiliation. From 30 October 1935, the breast-eagle was embroidered in white cotton on a *feldgrau* backing; from 19 June 1937 it was on a bluish dark-green backing. Embroidery changed to silver-grey on 5 February 1939, and on 4 June 1940 to mouse-grey on feldgrau backing. NCOs wore 9mm wide bright aluminium 'single-diamond' pattern yarn braid introduced 10 September 1935, or silver-grey artificial silk braid, on the front and lower edge of the field tunic collar.

The M1933 pointed *feldgrau* cloth shoulder-straps without branch colour piping changed to *feldgrau* facing-cloth on 10 December 1934 and to bluish dark-green facing-cloth on 10 September 1935. They were replaced on 26 November 1938 by rounded bluish dark-green facing-cloth shoulder-straps with branch colour piping around the outer edges as worn on the field greatcoat, and on 18 March 1939 further production of the old model straps was discontinued. For shoulder-strap and sleeve rank insignia see Table 3.

On 25 April 1940 NCO collar and shoulder-strap braid of mouse-grey artificial silk or cellulose-fibre wool was introduced, and in May 1940 the bluish-green facing-cloth collars and shoulder-straps were replaced by *feldgrau* uniform cloth, but these changes were not implemented until after the fall of France.

The **other ranks' dress greatcoat**, introduced 10 September 1935, was officer pattern but made of lesser quality *feldgrau* cloth. The shoulder-straps were of bluish dark-green facing-cloth with branch colour piping around the outer edges. The bluish dark-green facing-cloth collar was always plain.

The stone-grey trousers had 2mm branch colour piping when worn with the *Waffenrock*. The trousers were plain when worn with the field tunic, and in May 1940 the colour changed to *feldgrau* cloth. The traditional black leather hobnailed marching-boots, nicknamed *Knobelbecher* – 'dice-shakers' – were 35-39cm high from heel to ankle. They were shortened to 32-34cm on 9 November 1939 to save material.

The **M1936 marksman's lanyard**, introduced 29 June 1936 and awarded by the company commander, distinguished 12 levels of marksmanship. Award 1 consisted of a matt aluminium plaited cord with an aluminium Wehrmacht eagle on a shield, replaced in 1939 by an aluminium eagle above crossed swords on a shield all in a small wreath, suspended from the right shoulder-strap, hooked to the second tunic button. One to three aluminium acorns at the lower end designated Awards 2-4. For Awards 5-8 the M1939 badge with a larger wreath replaced the shield, and Awards 9-12 had this same badge in gilt. From 16 December 1936 artillery gunners wore the badge with artillery-shells instead of acorns.

The **other ranks' black leather belt** had a rectangular dress-quality bright aluminium pebbled buckle with the Wehrmacht eagle in a wreath with the *Gott mit uns* ('God is with us') motto, introduced 24 January 1936. The **84/98 service bayonet**, introduced in 1898, was carried in a blued steel sheath suspended from the belt by a black leather bayonet-frog. The standard ammunition pouches were of smooth or grained black leather with matt-grey aluminium fittings.

Formal and informal uniforms for other ranks

The Walking-Out Uniform for other ranks was the same as the Parade Uniform, except that the M1935 peaked cap replaced the helmet, standard black lace-up shoes the marching-boots, and ribbons the medals. The sword, Y-straps, ammunition-pouches and rifle were omitted.

The **other ranks' peaked cap**, in *feldgrau* tricot, introduced 10 September 1935, preserved the traditional 'plate' style, although privately purchased caps often took the officers' 'saddle' style.

An Artillery Wachtmeister acting as a battery sergeant major (*Hauptwachtmeisterdiensttuer*), wearing the M1935 service uniform with M1935 other ranks' field cap. Note his double cuff braids, indicating his appointment, and the lack of the usual report book stuffed into the front of his tunic. He wears a 1939 Iron Cross 2nd Class ribbon and the bronze SA Defence-Badge. France, May 1940. (Friedrich Herrmann)

Major Eberhardt Rodt (left) and Hauptmann Finster (right) in the Corn Market, Ghent, 20 May 1940 wearing the M1935 officers' field uniform, confer in a 4 x 2 Wanderer WII staff car. Finster is wearing the M1938 officers' field cap, a 1914 Iron Cross 2nd Class button-ribbon with 1939 bar, and the 1939 Iron Cross 1st Class. (Josef Charita)

Otherwise it was exactly the same as for the officers' cap, except for the 1.5cm wide patent leather or vulcanised fibre chin-strap with two black metal buckles, fixed to the cap with two 12mm smooth black lacquered buttons.

The Reporting Uniform consisted of the peaked cap, field tunic with ribbons and field-quality insignia, plain trousers and marching-boats, no field greatcoat, black belt with bayonet and bayonet-knot and marksman's lanyard.

Training and barracks uniforms for other ranks

The Service Uniform for technical and senior NCOs consisted of the peaked cap, field tunic with ribbons, M1935 field greatcoat, trousers and marching-boots, black belt with pistol and holster and grey suede gloves. Junior NCOs wore the helmet instead or the M1935 other ranks' field cap instead of the service-cap, and Y-straps, ammunition pouches and a bayonet instead of the pistol and holster. Junior NCOs also wore grey suede gloves.

The **other ranks' field greatcoat**, introduced 10 September 1935, was identical to the officers' version but was of lesser quality and the insignia was other ranks' field-quality.

The M1935 **other ranks' field cap**, introduced 10 September 1935, resembled the later M1938 officers' field cap, and was developed from the M1934 cap of 24 March 1934. It was made of *feldgrau* cloth with a *feldgrau* flap, and the eagle and swastika and national cockade was embroidered in white cotton on a *feldgrau* backing from 30 October 1935, and on a bluish dark-green backing from 19 June 1937. Embroidery changed to silver-grey on 5 February 1939, and on 4 June 1940 to mouse-grey on *feldgrau* backing. The cockade was enclosed by a 4mm woollen branch colour chevron, point-up.

For the Undress Uniform NCOs and men wore the peaked cap, the field tunic with ribbons, plain trousers and marching-boots, the field greatcoat if ordered, and the black belt with bayonet. NCOs wore grey

CEREMONIAL UNIFORMS
1: Oberstleutnant, Panzerregiment 8, full ceremonial uniform, Böblingen, Germany, July 1939
2: Hauptwachtmeister, Gebirgsartillerieregiment 79, parade uniform, Garmisch-Partenkirchen, Germany, July 1939
3: Fahnenjunker-Gefreiter, III (Jäg)/ Infanterieregiment 83, walking-out uniform, Hirschberg, Germany, July 1939

A

THE POLISH CAMPAIGN
1: Generalleutnant, 14.Infanteriedivision, field
   uniform, Lublin, Poland, September 1939
2: Hauptmann i.G., 14.Infanteriedivision, field uniform,
   Lublin, Poland, September 1939
3: Stabsgefreiter, Reiterregiment 2, field uniform, Rozan, Poland,
   September 1939

BLITZKRIEG RIFLE SECTION
1: Unteroffizier, Infanterieregiment 96, field uniform, Chelmo, Poland, September 1939
2: Obergefreiter, Infanterieregiment 96, field uniform, Chelmo, Poland, September 1939
3: Schütze, Infanterieregiment 96, field uniform, Chelmo, Poland, September 1939

DENMARK AND NORWAY
1: Unterfeldwebel, Divisional Staff, 198.Infanteriedivision, field uniform, Copenhagen, Denmark, April 1940
2: Sanitätsobergefreiter, Sanitätskompanie 1/234, field uniform, Kristiansand, Norway, April 1940
3: Oberleutnant, Gebirgsjägerregiment 138, field uniform, Narvik, Norway, May 1940

NETHERLANDS AND BELGIUM
1: Leutnant, Aufklärungsabteilung 254, field uniform, Breda, Netherlands, May 1940
2: Oberschütze, Infanterieregiment 49, field uniform, Namur, Belgium, May 1940
3: Gefreiter, Pionierbataillon 30, River Meuse, Belgium, May 1940

THE BATTLE OF FRANCE (1)
1: **Major, Panzerregiment 25, field uniform, Cambrai, France, May 1940**
2: **Panzerschütze, Panzeraufklärungsabteilung 5, field uniform, Aisne, France, May 1940**
3: **Hauptmann, Infanterieregiment (mot.)** *Großdeutschland,* field uniform, Stonne, France, May 1940

F

THE BATTLE OF FRANCE (2)

1: Oberschirrmeister, Panzerpionierbataillon 37, field uniform, Besançon, France, June 1940
2: Schütze, Infanterieregiment 154, field uniform, De Panne, Belgium, June 1940
3: Unteroffizier, Infanterieregiment (mot.) 66, fatigue uniform, Amiens, France, June 1940

THE ARMY OF OCCUPATION
1: Unteroffizier, Verkehrsregelungsbataillon 754, field uniform, Arras, France, July 1940
2: Generalmajor, 215.Infanteriedivision, service uniform, Chaumont, France, September 1940
3: Obergefreiter, Oberfeldkommandantur 672, guard uniform, Brussels, Belgium, September 1940

suede gloves and technical and senior NCOs the pistol and holster, the only field equipment carried with this uniform.

The Guard Uniform consisted of the helmet or field cap, field tunic with ribbons and plain trousers with marching-boots (*Waffenrock* with piped trousers for Guards of Honour), field greatcoat if ordered, black belt, bayonet and marksman's lanyard. Technical and senior NCOs had a sword or a pistol and holster, junior NCOs and men Y-straps and ammunition-pouches. All NCOs had grey suede gloves.

Field and fatigue uniforms for other ranks

The field uniform consisted of the helmet or field cap, field tunic with ribbons, field greatcoat if ordered, plain trousers and marching-boots. All NCOs had grey suede gloves.

Technical and senior NCOs carried a pistol and holster, and other NCOs acting as infantry platoon leaders carried the riflemen's field equipment with the map-case and, if equipped with a submachine gun, two olive-green canvas M1938 magazine pouches. Other infantry NCOs and men carried the standard riflemen's field equipment.

A ten-man rifle-section had an Unteroffizier as section leader, a Gefreiter as deputy, a light machine gun team with three Schützen (gunners), and five riflemen. The section leader wore the platoon leader's equipment, but was not normally issued with a submachine gun until 1941. The First Gunner, the machine gunner, operating the LMG34 light machine gun introduced in 1936, carried a pistol and holster instead of ammunition-pouches on his left front hip; and on his right front hip he had a black-leather spares-pouch. The Second Gunner, also the replacement machine gunner, carried standard riflemen's equipment with a pistol and holster instead of one set of ammunition-pouches; four 50-round ammunition drums, a 300-round ammunition box, and a sheet-metal barrel protector with one or two spare barrels. The deputy section leader, ordinary riflemen and the Third Gunner wore standard riflemen's equipment. Gunner 3 also carried two ammunition-boxes.

Officers in M1935 field uniform hold an impromptu meeting in Lichtervelde, Belgium, May 1940. Note the M1934 field cap worn by three officers and the leather greatcoat worn by the Major (2nd left). The Hauptmann (2nd right) is saluting before shaking the hand of the Major (1st right). (Josef Charita)

The **white drill fatigue uniform** was usually worn by enlisted men and only rarely by NCOs. It consisted of the M1934 field cap, M1933 fatigue tunic, fatigue-trousers introduced 1 April 1933, black belt and marching-boots. The tunic, made of cream or off-white cotton herringbone twill, had two patch side-pockets and five matt-grey painted pebbled buttons. Badges were confined to the special rank insignia described below. In 1940 the off-white colour was replaced on 12 February 1940 by a more practical mid-green, called 'reed-green'.

Tank crew uniforms

The M1934 black uniform was closely associated with the Panzer branch, but initially only tank-crews were authorised to wear it. Later, units of other branches in Panzer divisions were allowed to wear this prestigious uniform: signals battalions from 2 April 1937, artillery regiments from mid-1938, armoured reconnaissance battalions in March 1940, and on 10 May 1940 armoured engineer battalions. However, unauthorised personnel, such as general-officers, staff officers and members of unit staffs such as doctors, paymasters and company sergeant-majors, unofficially adopted the uniform. The colour, the distinctive double-breasted jacket and the collar patch skulls were intended to evoke the prestige of the Imperial German Cavalry.

The black uniform, introduced 12 November 1934, could be worn on all occasions except ceremonial. It consisted of the standard M1934 padded beret, later replaced by the M1940 field cap; a dark-grey tricot pullover shirt and black tie; the M1934 field jacket; M1934 field trousers and black lace-up shoes.

The **padded beret** was made of thick felt or red rubber sponge covered in black wool. From 30 October 1935 officers wore an eagle and swastika in bright aluminium bullion on the front of the beret, other ranks the badge in matt silver-grey machine-woven cotton thread, above a white cotton thread, later matt silver-grey machine-woven cotton thread, cockade and wreath, all insignia on a black backing. The beret proved too cumbersome in armoured vehicles, and on 27 March 1940 it

A motorcycle combination of a Military Police Traffic Control Battalion leads a convoy of trucks in France. Both riders are wearing the M1934 rubberised field greatcoat but with minimal equipment. The driver has slung his Karabiner 98k rifle over his shoulder, and wears the M1938 gas mask canister across his chest. His passenger carries a signal-baton. Note the divisional signs on the sidecar and the WH (*Wehrmacht-Heer*) number plate. May 1940. (Brian Davis Collection)

A dispatch-rider in the street of a town in German-occupied Flanders in May 1940. He is wearing the M1934 rubberised field greatcoat with an M1935 dispatch-case and has slung his M1938 gas mask canister on his chest, in order not to constrict his rear-passenger on his motorcycle. (ECPA)

began to be replaced by the M1940 officers' black field cap and the M1940 other ranks' black field cap. These caps were identical to the M1938 and M1934 *feldgrau* versions, but were in black cloth, with the eagle and cockade on a black cloth backing. Many officers and NCOs also favoured the *feldgrau* officers' M1935 peaked cap, M1934 peaked field cap or M1938 field cap, or other ranks' M1935 peaked cap or M1934 field cap.

The black wool double-breasted hip-length Panzer **field jacket** had a wide collar, with a 2mm branch colour facing-cloth piping, and wide lapels. The fly-front was closed by four large black horn or plastic buttons, with three smaller buttons left exposed above. Officers wore a matt aluminium thread breast-eagle, other ranks a white cotton, later a matt silver-grey, machine-woven cotton thread breast-eagle, all on a black cloth backing. All ranks wore standard black cloth collar-patches with branch colour piping and a bright aluminium stamped skull. All ranks wore field-quality shoulder and sleeve rank insignia, with black cloth replacing the bluish dark-green facing-cloth for NCOs and men. NCOs did not wear bright aluminium yarn braid collar braid. The M1934 plain black trousers tapered at the bottom to give a bloused effect, and buttoned and tied at the ankle.

When worn as a parade-uniform, officers' jackets had aiguillettes and the M1935 brocade belt, while other ranks wore the marksmen's lanyard and black belt. On 17 October 1938 a distinctive **new marksmen's lanyard** was introduced for armoured troops. It featured a matt aluminium eagle above a tank in a small ring for awards 1-4, in a large oak-leaf wreath for 5-8, in gold for 9-12, with, from 9 December 1938, aluminium acorns instead of shells. In the field all ranks wore a leather belt with a pistol and holster.

Special uniforms for other branches

General Staff officers wore bright aluminium collar and cuff-braids on the *Waffenrock* and matt aluminium thread collar-patches on the field tunic in the traditional *Kolben* pattern, whilst *OKW* and *OKH* officers wore the same insignia in bright gold thread on the *Waffenrock* and matt gold thread on the field tunic. These officers also wore general-officers' trouser and breeches pipings and braids in crimson facing-cloth on all uniforms.

Instead of the field cap, **Mountain Troops** wore the peaked mountain-cap used by German and Austro-Hungarian troops in the First World War – mountain troops were recruited heavily from Austria. The standard model, introduced about 1930, was in *feldgrau* cloth with a flap secured by two 12mm matt grey painted buttons, matt gold for general-officers. The eagle and cockade insignia was the same as for the M1938 officers' and M1934 other ranks' field caps, but officers did not adopt the aluminium and gold crown and flap pipings until 3 October 1942.

TABLE 2 RANKS OF THE GERMAN ARMY 1 SEPTEMBER 1939 – 9 MAY 1945

(omitting Army Officials; *Sonderführer;* Bandsmen NCOs and Men; Officer Candidates and *Osttruppen*)

Rank class	Rank (Staff & Infantry)	Command (Infantry)	Rank variants (other arms)	British Army
OFFIZIERE (officers)				
Reichsmarschall	—	—	Reichsmarschall des Großdeutschen Reiches[1]	—
Generale (*General officers*)	Generalfeldmarschall	Army Group	—	Field-Marshal
	Generaloberst[2]	Army, Army Group	—	General
	General der... Infanterie, Gebirgstruppe[12]	Corps, Army	General der... Kavallerie[13]/Panzertruppen[17]/ Artillerie[21]/Pioniere[24]/Nachrichtentruppe[28] Generaloberstabsarzt[32] Generaloberstabsveterinär[33] Generaloberstabsrichter[34] Generaloberstabsintendant[35]	Lieut. General
	Generalleutnant	Division, Corps	Generalstabsarzt[32] Generalstabsveterinär[33] Generalstabsrichter[34] Generalstabsintendant[35]	Major General
	Generalmajor	Brigade, Division	Generalmajor (W)[23]/(Ing)[27] Generalarzt[32] Generalveterinär[33] Generalrichter[34] Generalintendant[35]	Brigadier
Stabsoffiziere (*Field officers*)	Oberst	Regiment	Oberst i.G.[7]/(W)[23]/(Ing)[27] Oberstarzt[32] Oberstveterinär[33] Oberstrichter[34] Oberstintendant[35]	Colonel
	Oberstleutnant	Battalion, Regiment.	Oberstleutnant i.G.[7]/(W)[23]/(Ing)[27] Oberfeldarzt[32] Oberfeldveterinär[33] Oberfeldrichter[34] Oberfeldintendant[35]	Lieut.Colonel
	Major	Battalion	Major i.G.[7]/(W)[23]/(Ing)[27] Oberstabsarzt[32] Oberstabsveterinär[33] Oberstabsrichter[34] Oberstabsintendant[35]	Major
Hauptleute und Rittmeister (*Captains*)	Hauptmann	Company, Battalion.	Hauptmann i.G.[7]/(W)23/(Ing)[27] Rittmeister[14] Stabsarzt[32] Stabsveterinär[33] Stabsrichter[34] Stabszahlmeister[35]	Captain
Leutnante (*Subalterns*)	Oberleutnant	Platoon, Company.	Oberleutnant(W)[23]/(Ing)[27] Oberarzt[32] Oberveterinär[33] Oberzahlmeister[35]	Lieutenant
	Leutnant	Platoon	Leutnant(W)[23]/(Ing)[27]Assistenzarzt[32] Veterinär[33] Zahlmeister[35]	2nd Lieutenant
MUSIKMEISTER (Bandmaster Officers)[3]				
Musikinspizienten (*Music Directors*)	—	Inspector of Music	Obermusikinspizient[8]	L/Col, Dir/Mus
	—	Inspector of Music	Musikinspizient[8]	Maj, Dir/Mus
Stabsmusikmeister (*Senior Bandmaster*)	Stabsmusikmeister	Regimental band	—	Bandm Capt
Musikmeister (*Junior Bandmasters*)	Obermusikmeister	Regimental band	—	Bandm Lieut
	Musikmeister	Regimental band	—	Bandm 2/Lt
UNTEROFFIZIERE (Non-commissioned Officers)				
Festungswerk- meister & Hufbe- schlaglehrmeister (*Technical NCO s*)		Instructor	Oberhufbeschlaglehrmeister[33] Festungsoberwerkmeister[24]	WOI(SSM 1cl)
	—	Instructor	Hufbeschlagmeister[33] Festungswerkmeister[24]	WOI(SSM 1cl)
Unteroffiziere mit Portepee (*Senior NCOs*)	Stabsfeldwebel	Platoon, CQMS (12 years total service)	Stabswachtmeister[15] Sanitätsstabsfeldwebel[32]	WOII(RQMS)
	Hauptfeldwebel[4]	Company Serjeant Major	Hauptwachtmeister[15] Sanitätshauptfeldwebel[32]	WOII(CSM)
	Oberfeldwebel	Platoon, CQMS	Oberwachtmeister[15] Sanitätsoberfeldwebel[32]	CQMS
	Feldwebel	Platoon, 2ic	Wachtmeister[15] Sanitätsfeldwebel[32]	Serjeant

Rank class	Rank (Staff & Infantry)	Command (Infantry)	Rank variants (other arms)	British Army
Unteroffiziere ohne Portepee *(Junior NCOs)*	Unterfeldwebel	Section (6 years total service)	Unterwachtmeister[15] Sanitätsunterfeldwebel[32]	Lance-Serjeant
	Unteroffizier. Oberjäger[11]	Section	Sanitätsunteroffizier[32]	Corporal
MANNSCHAFTEN (Men)				
Mannschaften *(Men)*	Stabsgefreiter (neuer Art)[5]	Section member (5 years total service)	Sanitätsstabsgefreiter (neuer Art)[32]	Lance-Corpl
	Obergefreiter mit mehr als 6 Dienstjahren	Section member (6 years total service)	Sanitätsobergefreiter mit mehr als 6 Dienstjahren[32]	Lance-Corpl
	Obergefreiter mit weniger als 6 Dienstjahren	Section member (2 years total service)	Sanitätsobergefreiter mit weniger als 6 Dienstjahren[32]	Lance-Corpl
	Gefreiter	Section member (6 months total service)	Sanitätsgefreiter[32]	Lance-Corpl
	(Obersoldat[6]) Oberschütze Obergrenadier[9] Oberfüsilier[10]	Section member (1 year total service)	(Obersoldat[6]) Oberreiter[16] Panzeroberschütze[18] Panzerobergrenadier[19] Panzeroberfüsilier[37] Panzerzug-Oberschütze[20] Oberkanonier[21] Oberpionier[24] Panzeroberpionier[39] Bauobersoldat[25] /Bauoberpionier[26] Oberfunker[29] Oberfernsprecher[40] Oberkraftfahrer[30] Oberfahrer[31] Sanitätsobersoldat[32] Feldobergendarm[36]	Private
	(Soldat[6]) Schütze Grenadier[9] Füsilier[10] Jäger[11]	Section member	(Soldat[6]) Reiter[16] Panzerschütze[18] Panzergrenadier[19] Panzerfüsilier[37] Panzerzug-Schütze[20] Kanonier[21] Panzerkanonier[38] Pionier[24] Bausoldat[25]/Baupionier[26] Funker[29] Fernsprecher[40] Kraftfahrer[30] Fahrer[31] Sanitätssoldat[32] Feldgendarm[36]	Private

1 A Wehrmacht rank, held exclusively from 19.7.1940-9.5.1945 by Hermann Goering as nominally the most senior officer in the German Armed Forces.
2 Generaloberst im Range eines Generalfeldmarschalls (Acting Field Marshal) was created in 1935 as the then highest Army rank (with 4 pips) but was never held by any officer.
3 Bandmaster Officers ranked between officers and NCOs. Bandsmen's ranks have been omitted due to pressure of space.
4 An appointment, not a rank, usually held by an Oberfeldwebel, but also by a Stabsfeldwebel. A Feldwebel, Unterfeldwebel or Unteroffizier in this appointment was designated Hauptfeldwebeldiensttuer (Acting CSM).
5 Stabsgefreiter, introduced 6.1.1928, no further promotions after 1.10.1934, reintroduced 25.4.1942 as Stabsgefreiter (neuer Art), providing an extra pay-grade.
6 A generic term, covering all the variations in rank-titles.
7 General Staff officers.
8 Attached to OKH.

9 15.10.1942 for infantry regiments.
10 12.11.1942 for selected infantry regiments.
11 Light and mountain infantry.
12 Mountain infantry.
13 Mounted cavalry.
14 Mounted cavalry, reconnaissance, motor & horsedrawn transport.
15 Mounted cavalry, reconnaissance, artillery, smoke troops, signals, war correspondents (until 24.1.1943), motor and horsedrawn transport, veterinary corps.
16 Mounted cavalry, cyclist reconnaissance, veterinary corps.
17 Armoured troops.
18 Armoured troops and armoured reconnaissance.
19 3.6.1943 for mechanised infantry.
20 27.10.1942 for armoured trains.
21 Artillery.
22 Artillery and Smoke Troops.
23 Ordnance officers.
24 Engineers.

25 27.2.1940 for pioneers.
26 11.10.1939 for pioneers.
27 Engineer specialist officers.
28 Signals.
29 Signals and until 24.12.1943 war correspondents.
30 Motor transport.
31 Horsedrawn transport.
32 Medical corps.
33 Veterinary corps.
34 1.5.1944 for judge-advocate officers.
35 1.5.1944 for administrative officers.
36 Military Police. For ranks Oberst – Gefreiter add '...der Feldgendarmerie'.
37 For Großdeutschland and Feldherrnhalle mechanised infantry.
38 12.1941 for artillery regts of Panzer divisions.
39 15.4.1940 for engineer regts of Panzer divisions
40 For Signals radio operators.

Mountain Troops also wore M1935 stone-grey (from 1939 *feldgrau*) ski-trousers with *feldgrau* ankle puttees and fawn, brown or black leather studded climbing ankle-boots. They occasionally wore the greenish-khaki double-breasted close-woven calico wind-jacket, probably introduced in 1925, with shoulder-boards and straps the only authorised insignia, and the M1938 hooded reversible water-repellent fabric white-*feldgrau* anorak. Mountaineering equipment included the M1931 greenish-khaki canvas rucksack.

The commando units of **Army Intelligence** (*Abwehr*) wore German or foreign uniform appropriate to the occasion. It is known that some *Abwehr*

TABLE 3 Rank insignia of the German Army 1 September 1939 - 9 May 1945

Staff and Infantry ranks are normally given, but are in brackets where the insignia illustrates a rank variant. Most Bandmaster Officer and both Technical NCO ranks are omitted, and insignia on camouflage and fatigue tunics are excluded.

1. Generalfeldmarschall
(Field Marshal)
(1.9.1939 – 2.4.1941)

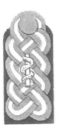

2. Generaloberst
(General)

3. General der
Infanterie etc.
(Lieutenant General)

4. Generalleutnant
(Major General)

5. Generalarzt
(General Major)
(Brigadier)

6. Oberst
(Colonel)

7. Oberfeldrichter
(Oberstleutnant)
(Lieutenant Colonel)
Judge Advocate
Service

8. Major
(Major)
Infantry Regiment
Hoch und
Deutschmeister'

9. Stabszahlmeister
(Hauptmann)
(Captain)
Administrative Service

10. Oberveterinär
(Oberleutnant)
(Lieutenant)
Veterinary Corps

11. Obermusikmeister
(Oberleutnant)
(Lieutenant)
Bandmaster

12. Leutnant
(2nd Lieutenant)
Army AA Artillery

13. Stabsfeldwebel
(WOII, RQMS)
21 Engineer
Battalion

14. Hauptfeldwebel
(WOII, CSM)

15. Oberwachtmeister
(Oberfeldwebel)
(Colour Serjeant)
11 Division Recce
Battalion

16. Wachtmeister
(Feldwebel)
(Serjeant)
Artillery

17. Unterfeldwebel
(Lance-Serjeant)
Infantry Regiment
'Großdeutschland'

18. Oberjäger
Unteroffizier
(Corporal)
Light Infantry

19. Stabsgefreiter
(Lance-Corporal
5 years total service)
24.4.1942 – 9.5.1945

20. Obergefreiter mit
mehr als 6
Dienstjahren
(Lance-Corporal
6 years total service)

21. Obergefreiter mit
mehr als 6
Dienstjahren
(Lance-Corporal
2 years total service)

22. Gefreiter
(Lance-Corporal
6 months total
service)

23. Obersoldat
(Private 6 months total
service)

24. Schüze/Grenadier
(Private) Infantry
Regiment
'Feldherrnhalle'

A good view of the M1935 field tunic worn by a Wachtmeister of Artillery in France, May 1940. His lack of field equipment and M1935 dispatch-case with modified fastener suggest assignment to the Regimental Staff. (Brian Davis Collection)

troops wore Polish, Belgian and Dutch uniforms during the Blitzkrieg period. From 13 November 1939 the inmates of the four Army **Penal Battalions** wore the standard Army uniform without any decorations, national, rank or branch insignia, and probably also a belt-buckle with a plain pebbled disc.

All ranks of mounted personnel of the **cavalry** or any other branch wore stone-grey (from April 1940) *feldgrau* riding-breeches with grey leather reinforcements. From 12 November 1934 motorcycle couriers and personnel in motorcycle reconnaissance battalions were issued feldgrau special clothing, consisting of a motorcyclist's protective greatcoat, a woollen turtle-neck sweater, long woollen stockings, and waterproof cotton gauntlets. The *feldgrau* heavy twill cloth M1934 greatcoat was rubberised on both sides and had a large *feldgrau* cloth collar, with *feldgrau* facings from 22 June 1935, bluish dark-green facings from November 1935 and finally back to *feldgrau* cloth in May 1940. Insignia was confined to shoulder-boards or straps.

Motorised Artillery and Motorised Infantry vehicle crews, Motor Transport drivers, and guards and sentries were issued the *feldgrau* waterproof M1934 surcoat. It was the same design as the field greatcoat, but ankle-length and cut generously at the waist to allow wear over a field greatcoat. **Smoke Troops** were issued protective clothing consisting of a dark-brown single-breasted leather tunic, trousers, gauntlets, peaked cap, face-mask and goggles.

On 26 August 1939 220 1,700-strong **pioneer battalions** were formed from members of the RAD (*Reichsarbeitsdienst*, the Nazi labour service) for construction duties along the eastern and western frontiers. Personnel wore RAD uniforms and insignia, changing to Army uniforms during the winter of 1939-40.

All **Medical Corps** personnel wore the M1937 white armband with a red cross on the upper left sleeve, introduced 6 March 1937. Orderlies also carried their first-aid kit in two smooth brown leather pouches.

The uniforms and insignia of Army Officials, including Chaplains and **Sonderführer** will be covered in Volume 3.

RANKS AND RESPONSIBILITIES

The rank structure of the German Army used a system established on 6 December 1920. Officers were divided into four groups: general-officers, field officers, captains and subalterns. By tradition the lieutenant-general rank indicated the officer's original branch of service, but in the case of officers of combat branches there was no differentiation in the insignia.

The first and second gunners of the section LMG team in field uniform operating their LMG34 machine gun in France in May 1940. Both soldiers have rubbed mud on their helmets as makeshift camouflage. Their M1935 field tunics have M1938 rounded shoulder-straps with unit numbers removed as per regulation. (Brian Davis Collection)

From 31 March 1936 Bandmaster Officers were grouped as a separate rank-class as Music Directors, Senior and Junior Bandmasters. Lacking power of command, they wore officers' uniforms and insignia, enjoyed officer status and were the equivalents of officers in the British and United States Armies. Music Directors, based at the OKH, were regarded as staff officers, while the Bandmasters supervised infantry, light infantry, cavalry, artillery regimental and engineer battalion bands.

NCOs were divided into three groups. Technical NCOs, established 23 September 1937, for senior instructors in the Fortress Engineers and later the Veterinary Corps; Senior NCOs, called 'sword-knot NCOs'; and Junior NCOs, or 'NCOs without the sword-knot'. The *Stabsfeldwebel* rank, introduced 14 September 1938 for NCOs re-enlisting after 12 years service, was initially held by First World War veterans. Hauptfeldwebel was not a rank, but an appointment, introduced 28 September 1938. He was the senior NCO in a company based at the company HQ and nicknamed *der Spieß* – 'the spear'. Usually an Oberfeldwebel, he out-ranked a Stabsfeldwebel (who could also be promoted to this appointment). Other NCOs receiving this appointment were designated *Hauptfeldwebeldiensttuer* (acting CSMs), but usually received rapid promotion to Oberfeldwebel.

The rank-class of 'Men' included all privates and lance-corporals, the latter, as experienced privates, constituting a larger proportion of this rank class than would be found in other armies.

Most ranks had alternative rank titles. Some, as in the Medical Corps, differentiated specialist officers without the power of field command. Others, such as *Rittmeister* or *Oberjäger*, preserved traditional titles.

Almost all officers held substantive ranks – the British system of acting ranks did not exist – so that German officers and NCOs often held higher commands than their British equivalent. It was therefore not uncommon for a Leutnant to be a company commander. While the first platoon of a typical rifle company was under a second leutnant, the second and third were often commanded by an Oberfeldwebel or Feldwebel. Promotions to the infantry ranks of Unteroffizier, Feldwebel and Oberfeldwebel depended on a unit's table of organisation, and were

TABLE 4 SELECTIVE LIST OF GERMAN ARMY BRANCH AND UNIT INSIGNIA
1 SEPTEMBER 1939 – 25 JUNE 1940

Units	In existence	Branch colour	Shoulder strap insignia	Other distinctions (comments)
Combat Troops - Staff (Kommandobehörde)				
General Officers (Generale)	1.9.1939 - 25.6.1940	Bright red	None	*Larisch* collar-patches, red trouser-stripes
Armed Forces High Command (OKW) officers	1.9.1939 - 25.6.1940	Crimson	None	Gold *Kolben* collar-patches, crimson stripes
Army High Command (OKH) officers	1.9.1939 - 25.6.1940	Crimson	None	Gold *Kolben* collar-patches, crimson stripes
General Staff (Generalstab) officers	1.9.1939 - 25.6.1940	Crimson	None	Silver *Kolben* coll.-patches, crimson stripes
5 Army Group (Heeresgruppe) Staffs	2.9.1939 - 25.6.1940	White	G (Nord, Süd, A, B, C)	
14 Army (Armee) Staffs	1.9.1939 - 25.6.1940	White	A / 1-10, 12, 14, 16, 18	
2 Armoured Group (Panzergruppe) Staffs	5.3.1940 - 25.6.1940	White	XIX, XXII	
33 Corps (Korps) Staffs	1.9.1939 - 25.6.1940	White	I - XXXIX series	
6 Motorised Corps (Korps(mot.)) Staffs	1.9.1939 - 25.6.1940	White	XIV, XV, XIX, XXII, XXXIX, XXXXI	
XVI Motorised Corps (Korps(mot.)) Staff	1.9.1939 - 25.6.1940	Pink	XVI	
Combat Troops - Infantry (Infanterie)				
143 Infantry (Infanterie) Division Staffs	1.9.1939 - 25.6.1940	White	D / 1-557 series	
431 Line Infantry (Infanterie) Regts.	1.9.1939 - 25.6.1940	White	1-664 series	
Line Infantry (Infanterie) Regt. 17	1.9.1939 - 25.6.1940	White	17	Brunswick skull cap-badge
4 Motorised (Inf.(mot.)) Division Staffs	1.9.1939 - 25.6.1940	White	D / 2, 13, 20, 29	
12 Motorised (Infanterie(mot.)) Regts.	1.9.1939 - 25.6.1940	White	5, 15, 25, 33, 66, 69, 71, 76, 86, 90, 92-3	
Infantry Regiment *Großdeutschland*	1.9.1939 - 30.9.1939	White	GD monogram	*Großdeutschland* title
Motorized Regiment *Großdeutschland*	1.10.1939 - 25.6.1940	White	GD monogram	*Großdeutschland* title
Hitler Escort (Führer-Begleit) Battalion	29.9.1939 - 25.6.1940	White	GD monogram	*Führer-Hauptquartier* title (12.1939)
3 Anti-Aircraft (Flak) Bns.	6.10.1939 - 25.6.1940	White	Fl / 31-2,46	
6 Light Infantry (Jäger) Bns. in Infantry Regts.	1.9.1939 - 25.6.1940	Light green	2 (I), 4 (II), 10 (I), 15 (III), 17 (III), 83 (III)	
4 Mountain (Gebirgs) Division Staffs	1.9.1939 - 25.6.1940	Light green	D / 1-3, 6	*Edelweiss* badges. Mountain cap
11 Mountain (Gebirgs) Regts.	1.9.1939 - 25.6.1940	Light green	98-100, 136-143	*Edelweiss* badges. Mountain cap
1 Commando Bn. (Bau-Lehr Bataillon zbV 800)	10.1.1940 - 31.5.1940	—	—	Any appropriate uniform
1 Commando Regt. (Brandenburg zbV 800)	1.6.1940 - 25.6.1940	—	—	Any appropriate uniform
Penal Bn. (Sonderabteilung I, II, IX, XIII) inmates	8.1.1940 - 25.6.1940	White	None (no shoulder-straps)	Uniforms without insignia
Combat Troops - Mobile Troops (Schnelle Truppen)				
1 Cavalry (Kavallerie) Division Staff	25.10.1939 - 25.6.1940	Golden yellow	D / 1	
4 Mounted (Reiter) Regts.	1.9.1939 - 25.6.1940	Golden yellow	1, 2, 21, 22	Cavalry breeches & boots
4 Mobile (leichte) Divisional Staffs	1.9.1939 - 25.6.1940	Golden yellow	D / 1-4	
7 Motorized Cav. (Kavallerieschützen) Regts.	1.9.1939 - 25.6.1940	Golden yellow	S / 4, 6-11	

SELECTIVE LIST OF GERMAN ARMY BRANCH AND UNIT INSIGNIA
CONTINUED

Units	In existence	Branch colour	Shoulder strap insignia	Other distinctions (comments)
4 Armoured (Panzer) Bns.	1.9.1939 - 25.6.1940	Pink	33, 65-67	Skull collar-patches, black
10 Armoured (Panzer) Division Staffs	1.9.1939 - 25.6.1940	Pink	D / 1-10 (6.7.39)	Skull collar-patches, black uniform
17 Armoured (Panzer) Regts.	1.9.1939 - 25.6.1940	Pink	1-8, 10-11, 15, 23, 25, 31, 33, 35, 36	Skull collar-patches, black uniform
1 Armoured Instruction (Panzer Lehr) Bn.	1.9.1939 - 25.6.1940	Pink	L	*1936 Spanien 1939* cuff-title
11 Motorised Rifle (Schützen) Regts.	1.9.1939 - 25.6.1940	Pink	S / 1-3, 12-4, 33, 69, 86, 110-1	
7 Motorised Rifle (Schützen) Regts.	1.9.1939 - 25.6.1940	Pink	S / 4, 6-11	(Ex-Motorised Cavalry Regts)
5 Motorcycle Recce. (Kradschützen) Bns.	1.9.1939 - 25.6.1940	Pink	K / 1-2, 6-8	
Motorcycle Recce. (Kradschützen) Bn. 3	1.9.1939 - 25.6.1940	Pink	K / 3	Dragoon eagle cap-badge
3 Armd Recce. (Panzeraufklärung) Bns.	1.3.1940 - 25.6.1940	Pink	A / 4-5, 8	
15 Mounted Recce. (Aufklärung) Bns.	1.9.1939 - 25.6.1940	Golden yellow	A / 54 - 187 series	
Mounted Recce. (Aufklärung) Bn. 179	1.9.1939 - 25.6.1940	Golden yellow	A / 179	Dragoon eagle cap-badge
32 Div. Recce. (Divisionsaufklärung) Bns.	1.9.1939 - 25.6.1940	Golden yellow	A / 1, 3-12, 14-9, 21-8, 30-2, 35, 44-6, 156	
Div. Recce. (Divisionsaufklärung) Bns 33, 35-6.	1.9.1939 - 25.6.1940	Golden yellow	A / 33-4, 36	Dragoon eagle cap-badge
10 Motorised Recce. (Aufklärung(mot)) Bns.	1.9.1939 - 25.6.1940	Golden yellow	A / 1-8, 20, 29	
148 Antitank (Panzerabwehr) Bns.	1.9.1939 - 25.6.1940	Pink	P / 1-672 (divisional series)	
144 Antitank (Panzerjäger) Bns.	16.3.1940 - 25.6.1940	Pink	P / 1-672 (divisional series)	
3 Mtn. Antitank (Gebirgspanzerabwehr) Bns.	1.9.1939 - 25.6.1940	Pink	P / 44, 47-8	*Edelweiss* badges. Mountain cap
4 Mtn. Antitank (Gebirgspanzerjäger) Bns.	21.3.1940 - 25.6.1940	Pink	P / 44, 47-8, 55	*Edelweiss* badges. Mountain cap
Combat Troops - Artillery *(Artillerie)*				
147 Artillery (Artillerie) Regts.	1.9.1939 - 25.6.1940	Bright red	1-557 (divisional series)	
4 Motorised Artillery (Artillerie (mot.)) Regts.	1.9.1939 - 25.6.1940	Bright red	2, 13, 56/20, 29	
4 Mtn. Artillery (Gebirgsartillerie) Regts.	1.9.1939 - 25.6.1940	Bright red	79, 111-2, 118	*Edelweiss* badges. Mountain cap
2 Mtd. Artillery (Reitende Artillerie) Bns.	1.9.1939 - 25.6.1940	Bright red	R / 1-2	Cavalry breeches & boots
1 Mtd. Artillery (Reitende Artillerie) Regt.	10.1.1940 - 25.6.1940	Bright red	R / 1	Cavalry breeches & boots
10 Armd. Artillery (Artillerie) Regts.	1.9.1939 - 25.6.1940	Bright red	73-6, 78, 80, 90, 102-3, 116	
40 Survey (Beobachtung) Bns.	1.9.1939 - 25.6.1940	Bright red	B / 1-36, 39, 40, 43, 44	
Ordnance officers (Offiziere(W))	1.9.1939 - 25.6.1940	Bright red	Gold crossed cannon	
3 Smoke (Nebel) Bns.	1.9.1939 - 30.9.1939	Bordeaux red	1, 2, 5	
9 Rocket Projector (Nebelwerfer) Bns.	22.9.1939 - 25.6.1940	Bordeaux red	1-9	
Combat Troops - Engineers *(Pioniere)*				
148 Engineer (Pionier) Bns.	1.9.1939 - 25.6.1940	Black	1-557 (divisional series)	
4 Motorised Engineer (Pionier) Bns.	1.9.1939 - 25.6.1940	Black	2, 13, 20, 29	
5 Mtn. Engineer (Gebirgspionier) Bns.	1.9.1939 - 25.6.1940	Black	54, 82, 83, 85, 91	*Edelweiss* badges. Mountain cap.
10 Armd. Engineer (Pionier) Bns.	1.9.1939 - 14.5.1940	Black	37-9, 49, 57-9, 79, 86, 89	Skull collar patches. Black uniform

SELECTIVE LIST OF GERMAN ARMY BRANCH AND UNIT INSIGNIA
CONTINUED

Units	In existence	Branch colour	Shoulder strap insignia	Other distinctions (comments)
10 Armd. Engineer (Panzerpionier) Bns.	10.5.1940 - 25.6.1940	Black & white	37-9, 49, 57-9, 79, 86, 89	Skull collar-patches, black uniform
220 Pioneer (Bau) Bns.	1.9.1939 - 22.12.1939	—	None (1-360 sorties)	RAD uniforms
220 Pioneer (Bau) Bns.	23.12.1939 - 25.6.1940	Light brown	1-360 series	
15 Fortress Pioneer (Festungsbau) Bns.	9.12.1939 - 25.6.1940	Black	19-314 series	
4 Fortress Engineer (Festungspionier) Bns.	7.2.1940 - 25.6.1940	Black	305-8	
Fortress Instructors (Festungswerkmeister)	1.9.1939 - 25.6.1940	Crimson	White Fp	Black & white shoulder cords
5 Railway Eng. (Eisenbahnpionier) Regts.	1.9.1939 - 25.6.1940	Black	E / 1-4, 68	
Engineer Specialist Generals (Generale(Ing.))	1.1.1940 - 25.6.1940	Bright red	Silver cogwheel	Larisch collar-patches, red trouser-stripes
Engineer Specialist officers (Ingenieure)	1.9.1939 - 25.6.1940	Orange	Gold cogwheel	

Combat Troops - Signals (Nachrichtentruppe)

Units	In existence	Branch colour	Shoulder strap insignia	Other distinctions (comments)
148 Signals (Nachrichten) Bns.	1.9.1939 - 25.6.1940	Lemon yellow	1-557 (divisional series)	
4 Motorised Signals (Nachrichten) Bns.	1.9.1939 - 25.6.1940	Lemon yellow	2, 13, 20, 29	
4 Mtn. Signals (Gebirgsnachrichten) Bns.	1.9.1939 - 25.6.1940	Lemon yellow	54, 67-8, 91	Edelweiss badges. Mountain cap
10 Armd Signals (Panzernachrichten) Bns.	1.9.1939 - 25.6.1940	Lemon yellow	37-9, 77, 79, 82-5, 90	Skull collar-patches, black uniform
1 Signals Instruction (Lehr) Battalion	1.9.1939 - 25.6.1940	Lemon yellow	L	1936 Spanien 1939 cuff-title
14 War Correspondent (Propaganda) Coys.	1.9.1939 - 25.6.1940	Lemon yellow	501-690 (Field Army series)	Propagandakompanie cuff-title

Supply Troops (Versorgungstruppen)

Units	In existence	Branch colour	Shoulder strap insignia	Other distinctions (comments)
608? Mot. Transport (Kraftwagen) Cols.	1.9.1939 - 25.6.1940	Light-blue	N / 1-557 (divisional series)	
920? Horsedrawn Transport (Fahr) Cols.	1.9.1939 - 25.6.1940	Light-blue	N / 1-557 (divisional series)	Cavalry breeches & boots
20 Mtn. Horsedrawn Transport (Fahr) Cols.	1.9.1939 - 25.6.1940	Light-blue	N / 79, 94, 111, 112	Edelweiss badges. Mountain cap
Medical Corps (Sanitäts) General-Officers	1.9.1939 - 25.6.1940	Bright red	Silver Aesculapius staff	Larisch collar-patches, red trouser-stripes
Medical Corps (Sanitäts) officers	1.9.1939 - 25.6.1940	Dark-blue	Gold Aesculapius staff	Red cross armband
166 Horsedr.Med. (Sanitäts) Coys-NCOs & men	1.9.1939 - 25.6.1940	Dark-blue	1-557 (divisional series)	Red cross armband; medical cuff-badge
? Mot.Medical (Sanitäts) Coys – NCOs & men	1.9.1939 - 25.6.1940	Dark-blue	1-557 (divisional series)	Red cross armband; medical cuff-badge
166 Field Hospitals (Feldlazarette) – NCOs & men	1.9.1939 - 25.6.1940	Dark-blue	1-557 (divisional series)	Red cross armband; medical cuff-badge
Veterinary Corps (Veterinär) General-Officers	1.9.1939 - 25.6.1940	Bright red	Silver snake	Larisch collar-patches, red trouser-stripes
Veterinary Corps (Veterinär) officers	1.9.1939 - 25.6.1940	Crimson	Gold snake	Cavalry breeches & boots
Farrier Instructors (Hufbeschlaglehrmeister)	1.9.1939 - 25.6.1940	Crimson	White horseshoe	Yellow wool shoulder-pieces
148 Veterinary (Veterinär) Coys – NCOs & men	1.9.1939 - 25.6.1940	Crimson	1-557 (divisional series)	Cavalry breeches & boots
27 Guard (Wach) Bns.	1.9.1939 - 31.3.1940	White	502-631 series	
10 M.P. (Feldgendarmerie) Bns.	1.9.1939 - early 1940	—	(None)531, 541, 551, 561, 571, 581, 591, 682-3, 685	Gendarmerie uniform; green armband
10 M.P. (Feldgendarmerie) Bns.	Early 1940 - 25.6.1940	Orange	531, 541, 551, 561, 571, 581, 591, 682-3, 685	Sleeve-badge & Feldgendarmerie title
10 M.P. (Feldgendarmerie) Traffic Control Bns.	26.10.1939 - early 1940	—	None (751-760)	Gendarmerie uniform: pink armband

Units	In existence	Branch colour	Shoulder strap insignia	Other distinctions (comments)
10 M.P. (*Feldgendarmerie*) Traffic Control Bns.	Early 1940 - 25.6.1940	Orange	751-760	Sleeve-badge & *Feldgendarmerie* title
201 M.P. (*Feldgendarmerie*) Troops	1.9.1939 - early 1940	—	None (1-557)	Gendarmerie uniform: green armband
201 M.P. (*Feldgendarmerie*) Troops	Early 1940 - 25.6.1940	Orange	1-557 (divisional series)	Green armband
Army Patrol Service (*Heeresstreifendienst*)	18.11.1939 - 25.6.1940	Any colour	Original unit	Adjutant's lanyard
Security Troops (*Sicherungstruppen*)				
24 Army Rear-Area Commanders (*Korück*)	1.9.1939 - 25.6.1940	White	K / 501-672 series, Norwegen	
14 District Commands (*OFK*)	1.9.1939 - 25.6.1940	White	K / 540-680 series	*Kommandantur* gorget?
49 Territorial Rifle (*Landesschützen*) Regts.	1.9.1939 - 31.3.1940	White	1 / I-3 (Army District series)	
21 Territorial Rifle (*Landesschützen*) Regts.	1.4.1940 - 25.6.1940	White	L / 22-183 series	
306 Territorial Rifle (*Landesschützen*) Bns.	1.9.1939 - 31.3.1940	White	I / I-XII / XVIII (Army District series)	
238 Territorial Rifle (*Landesschützen*) Bns.	1.4.1940 - 25.6.1940	White	L / 201-912 series	
33 POW Camps – officers (*Oflag*)	1.9.1939 - 25.6.1940	White	KG / I I / A-XXI / C (Army District series)	
45 POW Camps – NCO's & men (*Stalag*)	1.9.1939 - 25.6.1940	White	KG / I / A-XXI / E (Army District series)	
Army Officials (*Heeresbeamten*) – dark-green underlay (except chaplains) Special rank insignia				
Court Martial (*Reichskriegsgericht*) Generals	1.9.1939 - 25.6.1940	Bright red	None	*Larisch* collar-patches, green stripes
Court Martial (*Reichskriegsgericht*) Officials	1.9.1939 - 25.6.1940	Bordeaux red	None	
District Administration (*Intendantur*) Generals	1.9.1939 - 25.6.1940	Bright red	Silver HV	*Larisch* collar-patches, green stripes
District Administration (*Intendantur*) Officials	1.9.1939 - 25.6.1940	Bright red	Gold HV	
Paymaster (*Zahlmeister*) Officials	1.9.1939 - 25.6.1940	White	Gold HV	
Field Postal Service (*Feldpost*) Generals	1.9.1939 - 25.6.1940	Lemon yellow	Silver FP	*Larisch* collar-patches, green stripes
166 Field Post (*Feldpost*) Offices	1.9.1939 - 25.6.1940	Lemon-yellow	Gold FP (1-557 divisional series)	
37 Field Sec.Pol. (*Geheime Feldpolizei*) Groups	1.9.1939 - 25.6.1940	Light blue	Gold GFP (1-637 series)	
Chaplain-General (*Feldbischof*)	1.9.1939 - 25.6.1940	Violet	No shoulder-boards	Gold collar-patches, violet cap-band
Chaplains (*Pfarrer*)	1.9.1939 - 25.6.1940	Violet	No shoulder-boards	Silver collar-patches, violet cap-band
War Substantive Chaplains (*Kriegspfarrer*)	1.9.1939 - 25.6.1940	Violet	No shoulder-boards	Violet cap-band
Miscellaneous				
Music Directors (*Musikinspizienten*)	1.9.1939 - 25.6.1940	Bright red	Lyre	Gold *Kolben* patches: special shoulder-boards
Bandmaster officers (*Musikmeister*)	1.9.1939 - 25.6.1940	Branch colour	Lyre / Number of attached regt./bn.	Special shoulder-boards
Band NCOs & men (*Musiker/Trompeter*)	1.9.1939 - 25.6.1940	Branch colour	Number of attached regt./bn.	Shoulder 'wings'
Special Officers and NCOs (*Sonderführer*)	1.9.1939 - 2.3.1940	—	None (silver Aesculapius staff or snake)	Uniform of attached unit
Special Officers and NCOs (*Sonderführer*)	21.3.1940 - 25.6.1940	Grey-blue	None (silver Aesculapius staff or snake)	'Old Prussian' patches, grey-blue cap-band

France, June 1940. A Hauptfeldwebel in service uniform, displaying the double cuff braids and report book of his appointment. He has reversed his shoulder-straps to conceal his unit insignia. Note his Wehrmacht long-service ribbon. His relaxed attitude and lack of equipment suggest that the Battle of France is over. (Friedrich Herrmann)

the normal progression for a capable NCO. All other NCO and lower ranks were awarded on seniority. The rank of *Obersoldat* was held by a soldier lacking even the qualities for promotion to Gefreiter, while a Stabsgefreiter was an 'old sweat' unfitted for NCO rank. The ranks of officer candidates will be covered in Volume 2.

Rank insignia

Most rank insignia was manufactured in two versions – dress-quality for the *Waffenrock*, dress greatcoat and piped field tunic, and field-quality for the field tunic and field greatcoat.

For all uniforms **general-officers** wore dress-quality plaited shoulder-boards formed from two 4mm gold bullion (or, from 15 July 1938, golden-yellow 'celleon' thread) cords with one 4mm bright flat aluminium braid central cord on a bright-red branch colour facing-cloth backing. A Generalfeldmarschall had silver crossed stylised marshal's batons, other general-officers had 3-0 German silver or white aluminium pips 2.8–3.8cm wide. Branch insignia was in silver-plated aluminium. From 3 April 1941 all three cords of the Generalfeldmarschall were in bright gold or golden-yellow 'celleon' with miniature silver marshal's batons.

Dress-quality plaited shoulder-boards for **field officers** consisted of two 5mm wide bright flat aluminium braids on a branch colour facing-cloth backing and 2-0 pips 1.5cm, 2.0cm or 2.4cm wide, made of galvanically brassed aluminium, from 7 November 1935 gilt aluminium. During wartime they were made from golden galvanised or lacquered grey aluminium. Field-quality boards had matt aluminium, later *feldgrau* braid. M1935 branch insignia, introduced 10 September 1935, was, from 7 November 1935, made of brass-plated or gilt aluminium, and, during the war, of gold-coloured galvanised or lacquered grey aluminium or zinc alloy.

A tank-driver Gefreiter, exhausted by the Panzers' 'drive to the sea' through France in May 1940, enjoys a cigarette by his tank. He has not opted to wear his M1935 *feldgrau* field greatcoat over his M1934 special tank-crew uniform to protect it from the grime of battle. Note the drivers' goggles, civilian shirt and M1936 pullover. (Brian Davis Collection)

A classic view of a tank commander, wearing the 1934 special tank-crew uniform and the 1934 padded beret with tank commander's earphones. This officer is wearing the aluminium wire aiguillettes of a General Staff officer. France, May 1940. (Friedrich Herrmann)

Dress-quality shoulder-boards for **captains and subalterns** consisted of two 7-8mm wide bright flat aluminium braids placed side-by-side on a branch colour facing-cloth backing with 2-0 gilt aluminium pips and branch insignia as for field officers. Field-quality boards had matt aluminium, later *feldgrau* braid.

Music Directors wore field officers' shoulder-boards with two 4mm wide bright flat aluminium braids with a 3mm wide bright-red central silk cord, all on a bright-red facing-cloth backing (from 18 February 1943 the branch colour as for bandmasters) with a gilt aluminium lyre and 1-0 gilt aluminium pips. Senior and Junior Bandmasters wore shoulder-boards consisting of five 7mm wide bright flat aluminium braids placed side-by-side, alternating with four 5mm bright red silk braids on a branch colour facing-cloth backing (white, light-green, bright red or golden-yellow or black) with a gilt aluminium lyre and up to two gilt aluminium pips. Field-quality boards had matt aluminium, later *feldgrau* braid.

Technical NCOs had distinctive plaited shoulder-boards with devices and pips in white aluminium; these were made from grey aluminium or zinc alloy during the war. From 23 September 1937 Farrier-Instructors wore interwoven triple golden-yellow woollen cords with a double golden-yellow woollen cord edging all on a crimson branch colour underlay, a horseshoe and 1-0 pips. From 9 January 1939 Fortress Engineer Foremen wore the same shoulder-boards in black artificial silk with a white artificial silk inner edging all on a black branch colour underlay, with a cogwheel (from 9 June 1939 a Gothic Fp) and 1-0 pips. On 7 May 1942 both sets of shoulder-boards were changed to red, with bright aluminium and red interwoven cords, with a double red cord edging. Farrier-instructors had a crimson underlay and a horseshoe, fortress-engineers a black underlay and Fp, and 2-1 pips.

Dress-quality rank insignia for **senior NCOs** consisted of 3-1 bright aluminium pips (1.8cm, 2cm or 2.4cm wide) on M1935 bluish dark-green cloth shoulder-straps, with branch colour piping and edged on all sides by 9mm wide bright aluminium 'single-diamond' pattern yarn braid introduced 10 September 1935. Field-quality rank insignia consisted of the same pips and braid on the M1933, M1934 and M1935 unpiped, and M1938 and M1940 piped field shoulder-straps. 9mm silver-grey artificial silk braid was also worn, with grey aluminium and zinc alloy pips during the war, and from 25 April 1940 *feldgrau* matt artificial silk or cellulose-fibre wool braid. Branch insignia was of the same metal as the pips. A Hauptfeldwebel/Hauptfeldwebeldiensttuer wore a second 1.5cm wide bright aluminium 'double-diamond' pattern yarn braid above the cuff of the *Waffenrock*, and two 9mm braids on the cuff of other uniforms.

Junior NCOs wore the same shoulder-straps and braids as senior NCOs, the *Unterfeldwebel* wearing braid around the shoulder-strap, the *Unteroffizier* omitting braid across the base of the strap. Dress-quality branch insignia was fully embroidered in the branch colour on the shoulder-strap, while field-quality insignia was in branch colour wool or cotton yarn, and from 19 March 1937, also in artificial silk, embroidered in a chain-stitch pattern. Engineers' black and Medical Corps' dark-blue unit insignia were outlined in white chain-stitch on bluish dark-green shoulder-straps to render them more visible. During the war the embroidery was often full flat thin yarn.

Two soldiers in M1935 field uniform, the NCO (left) carrying an MP28/II Schmeisser sub-machine gun, guard British prisoners in northern France, May 1940. Note the general absence of field equipment – M1938 gas mask canister and M1931 canvas bread-bag and bayonet – but no Y-straps. (Josef Charita)

Other ranks wore the same shoulder-straps as junior NCOs, with branch colour branch insignia but without braids. The M1936 rank insignia consisted of chevrons, point-down, of 9mm NCO braid combined with embroidered silver-grey or aluminium thread pips (hand-embroidered bright aluminium bullion on privately purchased items). The insignia was sewn on to a triangular (circular for Obersoldat) backing of bluish dark-green facing-cloth, changed in May 1940 to *feldgrau* uniform cloth, and black for tank crew uniforms. This rank insignia was adopted on 25 September 1936 (with effect from 1 October 1936) and developed from the original *Reichswehr* system adopted 22 December 1920.

From 26 November 1938 rank insignia on the white and reed-green **twill fatigue-uniforms** consisted of 1cm wide *feldgrau* fabric and 'single diamond' braid with two thin black inner pipings. A Stabsfeldwebel wore a braid ring below two braid chevrons point-up, on each lower-sleeve; Hauptfeldwebel two rings; Oberfeldwebel, a ring and a chevron, Feldwebel, a ring only. Unterfeldwebel and Unteroffizier wore braid collar edging only. This NCO insignia was replaced by new sleeve rank insignia introduced 22 August 1942. Men wore chevrons of the same braid and *feldgrau* fabric, with braid pips sewn on to white or reed-green backings.

Branch and unit insignia

A German soldier's branch of service was indicated by a branch colour, worn on the collar and shoulder-board and shoulder-straps, and as cap, tunic and trouser pipings. The system of branch colours, a development of the regimental facing-colours in the *Reichsheer* of the German Empire, was established on 22 December 1920, continued, with comparatively few changes, until 9 May 1945.

An Unteroffizier, in M1935 field uniform, threatens French prisoners with his Karabiner 98k in northern France, May 1940. He wears a single set of ammunition-pouches and carries standard 6 x 30 binoculars, suggesting he is a section leader, and is sporting a civilian scarf against regulations. (ECPA)

Branch insignia comprised a symbol, or a letter in Gothic script, worn by certain specialised troops within a branch, above the unit insignia – an Arabic or Roman numeral, or, in the case of Army Schools, Gothic letter(s). There was a wide variety of such insignia, and so only a selection of the principal combat units is covered here.

Such precise unit identification aided personal and unit morale, but jeopardised field security and so, from 1 September 1939, troops in the Field Army were ordered to remove or conceal their unit insignia. Many troops covered the unit insignia on their field shoulder-boards and shoulder-straps with a *feldgrau* (black for Panzer units) shoulder-slide or wore their shoulder-boards/straps reversed. The branch insignia, which was less specific, was usually retained. Unit insignia could still be worn by the Replacement Army or by Field Army troops on leave in Germany. In fact, unit insignia was often worn in the field in defiance of these regulations. On 24 January 1940 3cm wide *feldgrau* shoulder-slides with branch and unit insignia in branch colour chain-stitch were introduced for NCOs and other ranks, but senior NCOs often continued to wear their white aluminium insignia. Insignia on dress uniforms not worn in the field, was unaffected.

The pre-war system of numerals on the shoulder-strap buttons of other ranks in regiments – blank for regimental staff, I–III for battalion staff; 1-14 for constituent companies – was replaced in wartime by standard blank buttons.

Certain specialised or élite units, or a few units carrying the traditions of regiments of the Imperial *Reichsheer*, wore special insignia, usually extra cap badges, worn between the eagle and swastika and the cockade, or, in a growing trend borrowed from the paramilitary *Sturmabteilung*, as sleeve-titles.

Table 4 gives a list of the principal units in existence from 1 September 1939 to 25 June 1940, with their branch colours, branch insignia, unit and special insignia. Existence of these units before or after these dates is not excluded, nor did all units necessarily see combat at this time.

From 2 May 1939 all ranks of mountain divisions wore insignia incorporating the alpine flower, the edelweiss, originally worn by German and Austro-Hungarian units in the First World War. A white aluminium edelweiss with gilt stamens was worn above the cockade on the peaked cap. A white aluminium edelweiss with a stem, two leaves and gilt stamens (war-time production used grey aluminium with yellow stamens) was worn on the left side of the mountain cap, Austrian personnel often adding a bluish dark-green facing-cloth backing. A machine-woven white edelweiss with yellow stamens, light-green stem and leaves within a mouse-grey rope wreath on a dark-green facing-cloth oval (after May 1940 *feldgrau*), was worn on the right upper sleeve of tunics and greatcoats.

Six infantry battalions also wore the light-green *Jäger* branch colour to preserve the light infantry tradition, but they remained infantry battalions – it was not until 28 June 1942 that specialised *Jäger* units were raised.

Two commemorative matt aluminium badges were worn by all ranks in certain regiments between the eagle and cockade of the service cap and, unofficially, on the field cap. From 25 February 1938 the 17th Infantry Regiment wore the Brunswick skull and crossbones to com-

memorate the Imperial 92nd Infantry Regiment. From 21 June 1937 the 3rd Motorcycle Reconnaissance Battalion, and from 26 August 1939 the 179th Mounted, 33rd, 34th and 36th Divisional Reconnaissance Battalions, wore the dragoon eagle, also called the 'Schwedt eagle' to commemorate the Imperial 2nd Dragoon Regiment.

The *Großdeutschland* Infantry Regiment was formed on 12 June 1939 from the Berlin Guard Regiment (*Wachregiment Berlin*) and developed into an élite unit. Defying field security, their insignia was worn throughout the war. The *GD* shoulder-board/strap monogram (introduced 20 June 1939) and a woven aluminium thread *Großdeutschland* and edging was worn on a bluish dark-green cuff title (introduced 20 June 1939). This was superseded for a short time in summer 1940 by a silver-grey woven Gothic-script *Inf.Rgt Großdeutschland*, which was worn on the right cuff of all uniforms. *Großdeutschland* personnel assigned to Hitler's field HQ, the *Führerbegleitbataillon*, wore a golden-yellow machine-embroidered, machine-woven or hand-embroidered (also found in silver-grey thread) Gothic-script *Führer-Hauptquartier* and edging on a black wool sleeve title.

From 21 June 1939 the Armoured and Signals Instruction battalions wore a gold machine-woven *1936 Spanien 1939* and edging on a madder-red cloth cuff title on the left cuff to commemorate their service in *Gruppe Imker* during the Spanish Civil War. From 16 August 1938 personnel of the newly formed war correspondent companies wore a machine- or hand-embroidered aluminium Gothic-script *Propagandakompanie* on a plain black sleeve-title on the right cuff.

The Military Police was formed on mobilisation on 26 August 1939 from 8,000 German *Gendarmerie*. Motorised three-company battalions were assigned to field armies, allocating a 33-man *Trupp* to an infantry division, a 47-man *Trupp* to an armoured or motorised division and a 32-man *Trupp* to a sub-district. Initially MPs wore their M1936 *Gendarmerie* uniforms with Army shoulderboards/straps and a medium-green armband with orange-yellow machine-embroidered *Feld-Gendarmerie*. This

Northern France, May 1940. A section LMG team in field uniform with the section leader (2nd left) watching for the enemy. The LMG34 is mounted on a tripod for use as a heavy machine gun. Note the machine gunner's improvised assault-pack, consisting of an M1931 mess-tin tied to the back of his belt with belt supporting-straps. (Brian Davis Collection)

49

was replaced in early 1940 by Army uniform with, on the left upper-sleeve the Police sovereignty-badge – a machine-woven or embroidered orange eagle and black swastika in an orange wreath (officers wore hand-embroidered aluminium thread) on *feldgrau* backing. On the left cuff was a machine-woven aluminium *Feldgendarmerie* on a brown sleeve-title edged in aluminium yarn, later machine-embroidered in silver-grey yarn. When on duty MPs wore the matt aluminium gorget with an eagle and *Feldgendarmerie* in aluminium on a dark-grey scroll. Traffic Control personnel wore the MP uniform without these three insignia, wearing a black cotton woven *Verkehrs-Aufsicht* on a salmon-coloured armband on the left upper sleeve. The Army Patrol Service, equivalent to British Regimental Police, wore the obsolete M1920 matt aluminium wire adjutant's lanyard on the field tunic and field greatcoat.

Music Directors wore staff-pattern bright gold, or matt gold, *Kolben* collar and cuff-patches, and from 12 April 1938 all Bandmaster Officers wore special bright aluminium and bright red silk aiguillettes on formal uniforms. On dress and field tunics regimental bandsmen wore M1935 'swallow's-nest wings' made of bright aluminium NCO braid and branch colour facing-cloth, introduced 10 September 1935, drum-majors adding aluminium fringes. Other specialist badges will be covered in Volume 2.

MEDALS

On 16 March 1936 the Wehrmacht **Long Service Decoration** was instituted as a cornflower-blue ribbon with, for the Army, a silver or gold eagle and swastika. Four or 12 years' service merited a silver or gold medal, 18 or 25 years, a silver or gold cross, and, from 10 March 1939, 40 years a gold cross with gold oakleaves on the ribbon.

Five pre-war **campaign medals** were awarded. On 1 May 1938, the matt silver '13 March 1938 Commemoration Medal', usually known as the 'Anschluss Medal', with a red, white and black ribbon, was issued to troops participating in the occupation of Austria. On 18 October 1938 the bronze '1 October 1938 Commemoration Medal' with a black and red ribbon, was issued for the occupation of Sudetenland, and on 15 March 1939, of Bohemia-Moravia. The bronze '13 March 1938 Commemoration Medal' with a red, white and green ribbon, was issued on 1 May 1939 for the occupation of Memel District. On 14 April 1939 the bronze, silver or gold Spanish Cross with swords and, the highest award, with diamonds, was instituted for service in the Spanish Civil War; it was worn as a pin-back cross on the right breast-pocket. Finally, on 2 August 1939 the bronze 'German Defensive Wall Medal' with a white and yellowish-brown ribbon was instituted for service building the Westwall – the 'Siegfried Line' fortifications on Germany's western frontier.

The most common military **bravery award** for courage in the field was the Iron Cross, reconstituted 1 September 1939 as a black and silver cross with a red, white and black ribbon. The Iron Cross 2nd Class was worn as a ribbon attached to the second button-hole of the field tunic, or as a small silver eagle, swastika and *1939* to the black and white 1914 ribbon. The Iron Cross 1st Class was a medal pinned to the left breast-pocket or as a larger eagle, above the 1914 cross. The Knight's Cross, instituted 1 September 1939, was worn from a ribbon around the neck. The War

Merit Cross, a bronze cross with a red, white and black ribbon, was worn in 2nd Class as a ribbon, or as 1st Class pinned to the left breast-pocket. It was awarded for merit or bravery in places other than the front line.

Other awards

On 22 May 1939 an oval aluminium pin-back **wound-badge** for the left breast-pocket was instituted for service in the Spanish Civil War, featuring a swastika and Spanish helmet on crossed swords within a wreath, manufactured in three versions – black, for one or two wounds; silver, for three or four wounds; and gold, for five or more, although not surprisingly, the gold was never awarded. On 1 September 1939 the badge, now with a German helmet, was introduced for the Second World War.

Four pin-back **combat qualification-badges** could be worn on the left breast pocket. The Condor Legion Tank Combat Badge, a bronze or white aluminium skull, tank and wreath, was instituted 10 July 1939. The Infantry Assault Badge, a white aluminium eagle, rifle and wreath, was issued from 20 December 1939, with a bronze version for Motorised Infantry from 1 June 1940. The Tank Combat Badge, a white aluminium eagle, tank and wreath, was instituted 20 December 1939 for tank-crews and medical support personnel, followed on 1 June 1940 by a bronze version for armoured car crews and medical personnel. The Engineers' Assault Badge, later the General Assault Badge, a white aluminium eagle, crossed bayonet and grenade and wreath, was instituted 1 June 1940, initially for assault engineers.

The Narvik Shield was awarded on 19 August 1940 for personnel who fought in Norway at the Battle of *Narvik*, 9 April–9 June 1940. It was a grey aluminium eagle above Narvik and a crossed edelweiss, propeller and anchor, worn on a *feldgrau* oval on the upper left sleeve.

Army personnel could also wear First World War medals and Nazi awards, such as the SA Defence Badge.

THE PLATES

A: CEREMONIAL UNIFORMS

A1: Oberstleutnant, Panzerregiment 8, full ceremonial uniform, Böblingen, Germany, July 1939 This battalion commander of Panzerregiment 8, which later fought in Poland, Luxembourg and France with 10.Panzerdivision, wears the regulation M1935 full ceremonial uniform with 'Flower Wars' and Nazi decorations, and the Army Long Service medal. The officers' M1935 sword-knot, made of *feldgrau* leather with an aluminium ball, introduced 7 November 1935, hangs from his privately purchased officers' sword, usually preferred to the M1922 issue sword introduced 17 February 1922.

A2: Hauptwachtmeister, Gebirgsartillerieregiment 79, parade uniform, Garmisch-Partenkirchen, Germany, July 1939 As the ranking artillery battery NCO, the Hauptwachtmeister was a formidable personality, wearing the double NCO cuff-braids of his appointment and his report-book stuffed into his dress or field tunic. He wears the marksman's lanyard, with artillery shells to denote the awards, and carries the officers' sword and sword-knot. As a member of the élite 1st Mountain Division, which later fought in Poland and France, he wears the Edelweiss arm-badge.

A3: Fahnenjunker-Gefreiter, III (Jäg)/Infanterieregiment 83, walking-out uniform, Hirschberg, Germany, July 1939 This conscript, accepted for officer-training, wears the other ranks' field tunic with officers' cuffs, branch colour pipings and dress-quality insignia as an alternative to the *Waffenrock*. The junior NCO bayonet-knot tied to the bayonet-frog is the only indication of his status.

B: THE POLISH CAMPAIGN

B1: Generalleutnant, 14.Infanteriedivision, field uniform, Lublin, Poland, September 1939 The commander of 14th Infantry Division, which fought in southern Poland with the 10th Army, and later in Belgium with the 6th Army, wears the leather greatcoat popular with general-officers over his field tunic. He wears the M1938 officers' field cap, carries the Walther PPK 7.65mm pistol on his belt, and has powerful 10 x 50 Zeiss binoculars.

B2: Hauptmann i.G., 14.Infanteriedivision, field uniform, Lublin, Poland, September 1939 General Staff officers were ranked *Generaloberst – Hauptmann im Generalstab* (Captain). This officer, the third divisional staff officer, the '1c' (Intelligence Officer), wears field-quality staff *Kolben* collar-patches and breech stripes, and the M1934 'old style' field cap. He carries a P08 Luger pistol in a hard shell holster and wears the cross-belt, which was abolished after the Polish campaign.

B3: Stabsgefreiter, Reiterregiment 2, field uniform, Rozan, Poland, September 1939 This cavalryman, a *Reichswehr* veteran promoted to Stabsgefreiter before the rank was abolished on 1 October 1934, wears the cavalry field uniform with reinforced breeches and riding boots. The 'lightning' arm badge indicates that he is a signalman in the regimental signals platoon. He carries the M1934 saddlebags for mounted personnel introduced 7 May 1934, and the M1934 Karabiner 98k, the standard German rifle. His regiment fought in Poland and France with 1st Cavalry Division.

A section of the *Großdeutschland* Regiment in M1935 guard uniform, France, June 1940. Members of this élite German infantry regiment wore the regimental cuff-title and shoulder-strap monogram on all uniforms, even in the field. Note the marksman's lanyards, as worn on this uniform, and the soldierly parade ground bearing of the troops. (ECPA)

C: BLITZKRIEG RIFLE SECTION

C1: Unteroffizier, Infanterieregiment 96, field uniform, Chelmo, Poland, September 1939 As a section leader this NCO is wearing the standard field equipment with a flashlight and 6 x 30 issue binoculars. He carries the Karabiner 98k rifle – section leaders were not normally issued submachine guns until 1941 – and a M1924 stick-grenade, known as the 'potato masher'. He has reversed his shoulder-straps to conceal his unit insignia and tied a thick rubber band to his helmet to secure his camouflage foliage. His regiment fought in Poland, Belgium and France with the 32nd Infantry Division. In the foreground lies a discarded Polish M1931 helmet.

C2: Obergefreiter, Infanterieregiment 96, field uniform, Chelmo, Poland, September 1939 This *Landser* ('German soldier') is the Section First Gunner, typically an Obergefreiter, with the 7.92mm IMG34 general-purpose light machine gun. He carries a machine gunner's field equipment: a P38 pistol in a hard-shell holster for close combat and an M34 spares pouch, a gas cape pouch across his chest in the prescribed manner, and two 50-round belts of 7.92 x 57 ammunition.

C3: Schütze, Infanterieregiment 96, field uniform, Chelmo, Poland, September 1939 The bulky M1934 backpack, introduced 10 February 1934, and the M1939, introduced 18 April 1939, was normally left with the unit's transport column, allowing infantrymen to fight in light order. The bayonet and bayonet-frog was strapped to the entrenching-tool on the left back hip, the mess-kit, camouflage shelter-quarter and gas mask canister worn on the lower back, and the bread-bag and canteen on the right back hip. The private carries a Karabiner 98k and has tied bread-bag straps to his helmet to fix camouflage foliage. In defiance of regulations he is displaying his regimental number on his shoulder-straps.

D: DENMARK AND NORWAY

D1: Unterfeldwebel, Divisional Staff, 198.Infanteriedivision, field uniform, Copenhagen, Denmark, April 1940 The 198th Division staff dispatch rider wears the M1934 motorcyclists' rubberised coat. He carries one set of ammunition pouches for his Karabiner 98k, the M1935 dispatch case and leather gauntlets. 'Square-lens' protective goggles are on his helmet. This division, raised in Bohemia-Moravia, occupied Denmark, taking the Danish flag as its vehicle-sign, before fighting in France.

D2: Sanitätsobergefreiter, Sanitätskompanie 1/234, field uniform, Kristiansand, Norway, April 1940 This Medical Corps orderly, assigned to a company of 163rd Infantry Division in Norway, wears the M1934 field cap and M1935 field greatcoat. He carries medical pouches on his belt, the gas mask slung on his back, and the larger, one litre, medical corps canteen at the front of his left hip. He wears the red-cross armband on his left upper sleeve and the medical qualification badge on his right cuff. He is holding a field dressing.

D3: Oberleutnant, Gebirgsjägerregiment 138, field uniform, Narvik, Norway, May 1940 This officer in 3rd Mountain Division in Poland and Norway, wears platoon leader's field equipment over his M1925 wind-jacket, with first model ammunition-pouches for his MP38 submachine gun, shown here with the stock folded. Against regulations, he retains his officers' brown belt, and carries a M1931 model rucksack, later superseded by a more utilitarian wartime model. Note the helmet's national shield, worn in the Danish and Norwegian campaigns despite orders on 21 March 1940 to remove it, and the distinctive 'T' form eagle and cockade worn on the mountain cap.

E: NETHERLANDS AND BELGIUM

E1: Leutnant, Aufklärungsabteilung 254, field uniform, Breda, Netherlands, May 1940 This Bicycle Squadron officer wears regulation platoon leader's field equipment, with the prescribed other ranks' black belt, with one MP38 ammunition-pouch and a M1935 dispatch-case. He wears the cavalry golden-yellow branch colour and the Gothic A for *Aufklärung* – 'reconnaissance' on his field shoulder-boards. His battalion invaded the Netherlands in May 1940 with 254 Infantry Division.

E2: Oberschütze, Infanterieregiment 49, field uniform, Namur, Belgium, May 1940 As Second Gunner, this infantryman wears one set of ammunition pouches for his Karabiner 98k and, for close combat, a P08 Luger pistol. He carries two 300-round ammunition boxes and an M34 single-barrel case on his back – LMG34 barrels were normally changed after 250 rounds of full automatic fire. This regiment fought in Poland, Belgium and France with 28 Infantry Division.

E3: Gefreiter, Pionierbataillon 30, River Meuse, Belgium, May 1940 This assault boat engineer has camouflaged his helmet with mud and wears simplified field equipment – an M1928 leather ammunition-pouch for his MP28/II *Schmeisser* submachine gun, a gas mask canister, bayonet

France, May 1940. An infantry Oberst in M1935 field uniform. The 'saddle-shape' of his M1935 officer's peaked cap is particularly noticeable. The distinctive officers' collar-patches, unlike those of other ranks, retained the branch colour piping throughout the Second World War. This officer is wearing the Knight's Cross, and his regimental number is concealed by a *feldgrau* slip-on shoulder strap. (Brian Davis Collection)

beret, a Walther P38 pistol in a hardshell holster and general purpose goggles. This battalion fought in Poland, Luxembourg and France with 2 Panzerdivision.

F3: Hauptmann, Infanterieregiment (mot.) *Großdeutschland*, field uniform, Stonne, France, May 1940 The regiment, which fought under direct *OKH* command in Poland, Luxembourg and at Dunkirk, was the first army unit with an élite unit cuff-band and shoulder-board monogram, which was retained in battle. This battalion commander, examining a discarded French M1935 tank-crew protective helmet, has removed the national shield from his helmet. He wears the Infantry Assault Badge in bronze for motorised infantry on his left breast-pocket, carries the M35 map-case with modified fastener, a P08 Luger in a hardshell holster, and 6 x 30 standard binoculars.

G: THE BATTLE OF FRANCE (2)

G1: Oberschirrmeister, Panzerpionierbataillon 37, field uniform, Besançon, France, June 1940 From 10 May 1940 engineer battalions of Panzer divisions wore black-and-white branch colour piping, instead of black, which was invisible on

An Unteroffizier of the 17th Infantry Regiment in Germany in July 1940 in walking-out uniform, wearing the Brunswick skull and crossbones commemorative cap-badge of his regiment. Note the marksman's lanyard, the Iron Cross 2nd Class button-ribbon and the typically pre-war style of shoulder-strap numerals. (Brian Davis Collection)

A Hauptmann in M1935 full ceremonial uniform poses with his bride on his wedding day in July 1940. He wears the Iron Cross 1st and 2nd Class, Wehrmacht long-service medals and 'Flower Wars' campaign medals, as well as the General Assault Badge. (Brian Davis Collection)

and entrenching-tool. He wears the Helmsman's qualification-badge in the aluminium machine-embroidered version introduced 7 November 1935, and, against regulations in a forward area, *feldgrau* slip-on unit shoulder-slides. He carries an assault-boat paddle and M1924 stick-grenades. His battalion fought with the 30 Infantry Division in Poland, Belgium and France.

F: THE BATTLE OF FRANCE (1)

F1: Major, Panzerregiment 25, field uniform, Cambrai, France, May 1940 This battalion commander wears the M1935 tank crew uniform and M1938 officers' *feldgrau* field cap, his *feldgrau* slip-on shoulder straps concealing his regimental number but not his rank. He carries the P08 Luger pistol in a hardshell holster, and 10 x 50 'short design' binoculars. His awards are the aluminium Tank Combat Badge on his left breast, and the 1939 Iron Cross 2nd Class ribbon from his first button-hole. He carries a tank-commander's headset with rubber earcups. His regiment fought in Belgium and France with 7 Panzerdivision.

F2: Panzerschütze, Panzeraufklärungsabteilung 5, field uniform, Aisne, France, May 1940 AFV-crews often wore their *feldgrau* field greatcoats to protect their black uniforms from dirt and grease, even though black was intended to disguise such soiling. This armoured-car driver wears the unpopular padded

M1938 gas mask canister above the M1931 bread-bag on the lower back, and the M1931 canteen on the right back hip.

G3: Unteroffizier, Infanterieregiment (mot.) 66, fatigue uniform, Amiens, France, June 1940 This member of the 13th Motorised Division, newly arrived in France, undertakes labouring duties in the M1933 white twill fatigue uniform. This uniform was already being replaced by the more practical reed-green, and junior NCO collar insignia was worn until 22 August 1942.

H: THE ARMY OF OCCUPATION

H1: Unteroffizier, Verkehrsregelungsbataillon 754, field uniform, Arras, France, July 1940 Traffic Control battalions were raised to regulate the swiftly advancing German road-traffic. Personnel wore police uniforms, adopting in early 1940 Army uniforms with orange branch colour pipings and a distinctive armband, but not the arm-badge, cuff-title and duty gorget normally associated with German Military Police. Although *feldgrau* collars, shoulder-straps and trousers were prescribed in May 1940, they were not general issue until 1941-2, and so this NCO, his battalion operating under *OKH* command in occupied northern France, still wears M1935 bluish dark-green facing-cloth collar and straps and stone-grey trousers.

H2: Generalmajor, 215.Infanteriedivision, service uniform, Chaumont, France, September 1940 The deputy commander of the 215th Infantry Division, on occupation duties with the 1st Army in eastern France, wears the officers' service uniform with the M1937 officers' piped field tunic and carries a Walther PPK 7.65mm Luger pistol in a hardshell holster. He wears the Iron Cross 1st Class on his left breast pocket, the 1914 2nd Class ribbon and bar on his second button-hole, and the Narvik Shield for service in the Norwegian campaign.

H3: Obergefreiter, Oberfeldkommandantur 672, guard uniform, Brussels, Belgium, September 1940 This soldier at the HQ of 672 District Command, covering Brussels, wears the guard uniform. It is a more formal field uniform with the marksman's lanyard and equipment limited to belt, ammunition-pouches, bayonet and scabbard. As a lance-corporal, with six years seniority and little likelihood of promotion to NCO rank, he wears the uncommon chevron and pip sleeve rank insignia worn until the end of the war by soldiers not promoted to the new Stabsgefreiter rank after 25 April 1942.

Luxembourg, 18 September 1940. A cavalry Wachtmeister in parade uniform without the usual belt, but with the steel helmet, which he has removed in favour of an M1938 field cap, as he tries to make friends with a local girl. Unlike most scenes of this type, this one does not seem to be stage-managed. He wears the Iron Cross 1st Class and seems to have been awarded the Iron Cross 2nd Class quite recently. Note the highly polished riding-boots. (Josef Charita)

their black uniforms. This reverted to black in 1941 when special *feldgrau* AFV uniforms were adopted. This Oberfeldwebel (Oberschirrmeister), supervising his company's technical equipment, wears his yellow wool embroidery trade-badge on a dark bluish-green facing-colour disc, with the aluminium wire edging denoting his NCO status. His battalion, formed 15 April 1940, fought in France with 1 Panzerdivision.

G2: Schütze, Infanterieregiment 154, field uniform, De Panne, Belgium, June 1940 The A-frame battle-pack, introduced 18 April 1939, was still comparatively rare in 1940, so infantry and assault engineers improvised, using M1939 black leather belt supporting straps to carry the M1931 shelter-quarter wrapped around the M1931 mess-kit. This infantryman, with the 58th Infantry Division in action in France and Belgium, wears the standard short entrenching-tool, bayonet, scabbard and frog on his left back hip, the

INDEX

(References to illustrations are shown in **bold**. Plates are shown with caption locators in brackets: e.g. **A1** (37).)